The voice of r

 The**inspirational**series™
Overcoming adversity and thriving

Teacup in a Storm
Finding my Psychiatrist
BY TOVA FEINMAN

We are proud to introduce The**inspirational**series™. Part of the Trigger family of innovative mental health books, The**inspirational**series™ tells the stories of the people who have battled and beaten mental health issues. For more information visit: www.triggerpublishing.com

THE AUTHOR

 Tova Feinman lives in Boston, Massachusetts and is a scientist by training. Tova studied chemistry as an undergrad, as well as biochemistry and toxicology in graduate school.

However, in her DNA, Tova is a writer. With published and soon-to-be-published essays like "Mania: The Hat, The 55lb Rabbit, and Dr. Rosen", "Manic at Sixteen", and "A Psychotic Depression Meets Academia", she writes about her experiences suffering from mental illness while navigating life.

First published in Great Britain 2018 by Trigger

Trigger is a trading style of Shaw Callaghan Ltd & Shaw Callaghan 23 USA, INC.

The Foundation Centre

Navigation House, 48 Millgate, Newark

Nottinghamshire NG24 4TS UK

www.triggerpublishing.com

British Library Cataloguing in Publication Data

A CIP catalogue record for this book is available upon request
from the British Library

ISBN: 978-1-911246-81-7

This book is also available in the following e-Book formats:

MOBI: 978-1-911246-84-8

EPUB: 978-1-911246-82-4

PDF: 978-1-911246-83-1

AUDIO: 978-1-912478-59-0

Cover design and typeset by Fusion Graphic Design Ltd

Project Management by Out of House Publishing

Printed and bound in Great Britain by Bell & Bain, Glasgow

Paper from responsible sources

www.triggerpublishing.com

Thank you for purchasing this book.
You are making an incredible difference.

Proceeds from all Trigger books go directly to
The Shaw Mind Foundation, a global charity that focuses
entirely on mental health. To find out more about
The Shaw Mind Foundation visit, **www.shawmindfoundation.org**

MISSION STATEMENT

Our goal is to make help and support available for every
single person in society, from all walks of life.
We will never stop offering hope. These are our promises.
Trigger and The Shaw Mind Foundation

Creating hope for children,
adults and families

*This book is dedicated to my daughter Katie,
a true miracle in my life.*

Trigger Warning: The book contains references to explicit sexual assault and eating disorders.

Disclaimer: Some names and identifying details have been changed to protect the privacy of individuals.

INTRODUCTION

The bond between patient and psychiatrist can be intense. It's a bond that needs to be nurtured and developed in baby steps, one therapeutic hurdle at a time. My relationship with my psychiatrist, Dr. Guterson, has been a long one, spanning over 20 years. Our clinical bond has been tested time and time again as Dr. Guterson has supported me in my recovery from bipolar I disorder and intense childhood trauma. My confidence in him as my psychiatrist is unshakeable. Dr. Guterson has become one of the most trusted people in my life.

Those of us with tortured minds have to face the fact that our road out of suffering is complex, and that it involves a great deal of commitment, both from ourselves and the physicians that we deal with. This can seem grossly unfair at times; if we were to break our arm and go to the hospital, there would be little delay in its fixing. An x-ray would be taken, bones set back into place, a cast administered, and we'd be on our way. But psychiatrists can't simply fix mental illnesses with something so simple as a cast. They deal with different tools – tools such as communication and trust – and these can take time to develop.

This is something I have had to learn, and I only hope that my decades with Dr. Guterson can provide hope for those still waiting for their recovery. I truly believe that, with the right psychiatrist, we patients can take back our lives.

Psychiatry freed me from a tortured past and a lethal illness. Now, I'm learning to claim the promise of a future that once seemed impossible.

Tova Feinman

CHAPTER 1

LIFE BEFORE DR. GUTERSON:

My story

I was a determined six-year-old, dangling precariously over the edge of a garbage dumpster behind my elementary school. I drooled, staring at the feast that lay just beyond my grasp. There was pudding, peanut butter and jelly sandwiches, peas, hamburgers, and brownies all laid out in front of me. All I needed was another foot of reach and the delicacies would be all mine. I had stopped feeling the hunger pangs in my stomach, but I couldn't get my brain to stop thinking about food. As I squirmed upside-down for a better reach, I heard a shout.

'Tova! What are you doing? Get out of there, you dirty girl!'

But I didn't want to get out of there.

I wanted pudding, but Mrs. Cooper was a frightening first-grade teacher. I tried to right myself as I pulled out of the dumpster, but instead I fell to the ground, my threadbare green plaid dress raised and exposing the previous night's shame. Mrs. Cooper glared at me and ordered me to stand up and turn around. Terrified, I tried to pull down my dress but the fabric got stuck in my underwear.

'Turn around, Tova, NOW!' the desiccated old woman bellowed.

I had no choice. I turned around, bare legs and buttocks exposed. Mrs. Cooper abruptly stopped screaming at me. As I quaked before her, she asked, 'How did you get hurt like that?'

I was truly baffled and said, 'I'm not hurt.'

Mrs. Cooper was incredulous. 'You are lying. Your legs and your bum are covered in welts and bruises. So, how did you get hurt?'

Rooting around for my courage, I turned and screamed, 'I'm not hurt! I don't get hurt, ever!'

The recess bell rang. I gave my dress one last yank, pulled up my stained knee socks, and ran to stand in line with the other children. Mrs. Cooper stared in disbelief as I whizzed past her, desperate to avoid her scrutiny.

*

As a child, I subsisted on a diet of trauma and terror, washing the bitter mixture down with my daily tears. My very existence depended on the decisions my stable of caregivers made for me, but that sacred trust was routinely violated. In the battle against their own psychological demons, they left me without protection, nurturance, and safety. The chaos of a childhood dominated by other people's untreated mental illnesses left me defenseless.

In the kaleidoscope world where reality was contorted by the psychoses of others – and where there was no safe space to find refuge – I clung to my only two childhood assets: my intellect and my innate certainty that G-d protected little girls. I used my intellect to create, in the safety of my own mind, a protected inner world to dwell in. That world was made up of the families I watched, with rapt attention, on the television programs that dominated the 1960s and 1970s. I relied on G-d for comfort when the brutality of the adult world intruded on my sanctuary. Early in my life, the Sabbath candle was my bridge to G-d.

I remember very vividly my first Shabbos, and the lifelong impact it would have on me. Stella, frail and world weary, stood before her silver candlesticks that Friday evening, waiting for 6.18pm. That time was just before the sun tucked below the horizon, and it signaled the beginning of Shabbos.

She struck a match at the sacred moment and, with an aura of reverence, lit all seven of her candles, one for every one of her children, living and deceased. The room flooded with light. The sweeping, circular motion of her gnarled hands mesmerized me as I leaned my bruised body into her fragile one. I listened in rapt attention as she sang a blessing in a language I did not understand but felt connected to somehow. The old woman took my tiny hand and whispered tenderly, 'Come sit with me, Tova.'

Battered but obedient, I cuddled up next to her. I stared at the flames rising up from the candles. Even at such a young age, I believed they were reaching for somewhere, some place mystical and sublime. The warmth emanating from the glow of the burning wicks was a holy warmth that melted away my suffering, at least in that moment, and beckoned me to snuggle, all the more, into Stella's frame. The woman turned to me, kissed my forehead, and softly said, 'Tova, G-d protects little girls.'

As I soaked in the holiness of the light, there was absolutely no doubt in my spiritually awakening mind that G-d did – and would indeed – protect me. I was a terrorized child with no human to turn to, but I found, in the light of Shabbos, a protector greater than any human guardian.

And I was right. G-d did come through for me. He gave me academic gifts and my inner safe space.

*

Years ago, I found this teacher's note while I was rummaging through a storage shed looking for a book to pack for college. It read:

To Whom It May Concern,

Tova is an extremely bright child. However, she has become quite a disruption in class. She stares out the window for long periods of time, totally unaware of where she is or what she is supposed to be learning. She has become the target of other students' nonstop teasing and yet shows no reaction to it. She is in danger of failing all her subjects if this behavior isn't addressed.

Mrs. Woolsey, Canton Elementary School, 3rd grade

Mrs. Woolsey's note perfectly summed up my childhood. She addressed it, "To Whom It May Concern" because she had no idea who would take on the responsibility for dealing with my "disruptive behavior". Then she assumed there would be someone who cared about me enough to talk to me about her concerns, when, in fact, there was no one. What my 3rd grade teacher was observing from the outside was the fact that I was encapsulated in my bubble on the inside. She was right.

I was totally oblivious to the world around me. It was deliberate. No amount of adult criticism would have had any effect on me. I was inside my safe zone and I wasn't going to engage the world unless I absolutely had to. She was also right that I was constantly on the receiving end of some pretty vicious bullying. However, she was wrong when she wrote that I had no reaction to it. I cared deeply. But my response was to burrow deeper inside my make-believe world, so that there would be no pain.

I did find a way to balance my love for academia with my need for safety as I got a bit older. I had such a thirst for learning that I was willing to emerge from my bubble long enough to soak in as much information as I could. I read constantly and studied intensely. In 8th grade I won an all-expenses-paid scholarship to a summer college program for advanced middle school students. I lived on a college campus for an entire summer, with no caretakers, no trauma, and no terror. I made friends (okay, two friends) and studied college classes like human physiology and psychology. It was at this program that I decided I wanted to go to medical school and become a psychiatrist. I wanted to cure psychosis. I decided someone had to take on the disease that had ravaged my childhood. Suddenly, at 13 years old, I found myself with a goal and a plan for the future.

What I also discovered during that summer was that I didn't need my inner world so much when I wasn't mired in chaos. I wasn't self-aware enough to understand that my bubble was my cloak of protection. I could wear it if I needed it and hang it up when in safety. Nothing threatened me that summer in 1974 and I matured, without my cloak, in huge strides and in just a few months.

*

With faith in G-d and the intellect He blessed me with, I endured and survived a dark childhood. But I had no way of knowing, as I made my exodus from the Egypt that was my childhood into the desert of my adulthood, what a battle I would have to fight to reach the promised land of true emancipation.

I entered my young adulthood a tumbleweed, blowing from university to university, graduate school to graduate school, even flirting with a medical school admission, without ever finishing anything more than my bachelor's degree and a graduate school degree I never planned to finish.

My undergrad experience was tumultuous. I attended two colleges, one of which I was driven out of by campus gossip. I was assaulted in my dorm room by a young man with religious delusions. Just when I thought I would never again be the victim of someone else's psychosis, there I was – at 3am one morning in 1979 – face-to-face with an assailant who called me Jezebel and compared me to a Moabite woman.

My assault became fodder for campus rumormongering, and so I fled the blather factory for a religious school half-way across the country. The dorms had bed checks, curfews, and a ban on men. I felt sheltered, and from within that cocoon I finished my bachelor's degree in chemistry. I applied to medical school and received an invitation for an interview.

However, simultaneously, I was drowning in my first deep and profound bipolar depression. I was carried through my senior year by one of my chemistry professors and my rabbi. My medical school interview was a disaster. In the middle of being questioned, I burst into involuntary sobs and found myself rocking, with my head buried in my hands. I walked out, never completing the interview. I was humiliated. My descent into bipolar disorder destroyed my 8th grade dream of becoming a physician. I was now directionless.

I belonged nowhere, to no one, least of all to myself. I was 23 years old – with no human ties I would admit to – and facing a future I couldn't find a place in.

I tumbled into Chicago one year and took a job as a research assistant, taking grad classes at the same time. The job and classes held my attention long enough that I stayed in one spot for over a year. One day, as I puzzled out my future in the graduate student lounge, a poster caught my eye. It said, "Join the Peace Corps, Make a Difference in People's Lives, Change Your Own."

All the neurons in my brain fired simultaneously. This was my answer. This was a giant neon postcard and on it was my destiny. Eight months later, I was on a plane to East Africa with 70 other volunteers for a two-year commitment, with no clue as to what I had undertaken. All I knew was that 10,000 miles would separate me from Boston, my childhood residence. For the first time in 24 years, I could breathe.

But I was grossly ill-prepared; not for my work or the culture, but for the changes that would take place inside my own psyche. I joined the Peace Corps to flee my tangled past, but all I managed to do was bunch those threads into one big jumbled knot.

It started innocently enough. We were a group of Peace Corps volunteers, swapping stories about home while in training – for four months – to live and work in a complex and ancient culture. As I sat in one of the mud-walled training huts one day, listening to the group reminisce about childhood escapades, a panic swelled in my gut. What was I going to say?

Should I sit silent? Should I leave?

I was in mid-alarm. I had no time to flee; I was next in the circle. So, from somewhere deep inside my inner childhood world came a story about a family vacation that was idyllic, adventurous, and pulled straight from a Brady Bunch episode. I regaled everyone with a tale of a trip to the Grand Canyon when I was eight. I talked about taking a burro down to the base of the canyon and how my dad rode protectively by my side for the entire descent. I described the panoramic view, the exquisite rock formations, and the sound of the Colorado River splashing with almost the echo of a giggle.

My ruse worked. My "memory" was met with head nods and "wows". From that moment on, I reinvented where I came from and how I grew up, based on the adventures from my beloved childhood television programs. I couldn't verbalize the truth about my life, so fantasy became reality as a substitute. I had found a new way to escape.

Peace Corps had – and still has – a persnickety attitude toward volunteers staying in-country indefinitely, so I stayed as long as I could, which was for three years. My future husband, Joe, left a year earlier. Joe had been my nearest Peace Corps neighbor and we'd begun a romance in our very remote corner of the Rift Valley.

It was now my turn to leave the volatile but protective cocoon of Africa. I had to go back to the U.S., and that meant going back to Boston. I couldn't travel there and bring my television family memories with me. I needed those "memories" to be unchallenged so that I could draw on them again if I ever needed them. I grieved at the cruelty of having to say goodbye to all those comforting "reminiscences".

I did stop in one country on my way back to the States, though: Israel. I hung out in Jerusalem for six weeks. I was desperate to reconnect with the G-d who had shepherded me through the abyss of my childhood. In Peace Corps, by living a lie, I had traded my principles for the illusion of safety. That reality shamed me. I needed redemption so I could reclaim my soul. I had lost it somewhere between tales of the Grand Canyon and a mother–daughter banquet.

There, at the Western Wall – just like with those Shabbos candles so long ago – G-d and I talked. I spent the next several evenings sobbing in my cot at the youth hostel. In the depth of my depression and shame, I was forced to cough up my ugly childhood memories like phlegm. Their return was a torment I didn't remember how to bear.

As my EL AL flight touched down in the U.S. in December of 1986, I instantly felt sick. Did I really have to go to Boston? But where else was I going to go?

I flew in and then flew back out days later, but this time I dragged more baggage with me than just my beat-up old duffle bag. Ultimately, I blew into Joe's backyard in the Midwest in January of 1987. I started yet another graduate school program, and Joe and I married in the fall of 1988.

I was no more capable of navigating the stresses of marriage than I was the stresses of life in Peace Corps. The three years I spent appropriating the plots of television programs to escape truth should have been a wake-up call to me that I was struggling with traumas too big for me to conquer alone. It took motherhood to roust me out of my delusion that I was just fine.

In October of 1990, I turned 30 years old. If you looked at me from afar, you would have seen a young woman who had absolutely everything she could possibly want. I was married to my best friend from my Peace Corps years, we were blessed with a precious newborn baby daughter, and we were buying our first home. Joe's career as a healthcare professional was taking off. My career as an analytical environmental chemist was on the fast track. We appeared to be the quintessential young professional couple.

However, if you looked just a little closer, you would have witnessed a woman coming apart at the seams. My marriage was not a holy union. We were each consumed by our own personal infernos. I was sinking into severe mental illness and he was ravaged by a prescription drug addiction that he confessed to me only after suddenly losing his job.

As Peace Corps buddies and traveling companions, we were completely in sync. As a married couple, we were the source of each other's destruction. Our daughter was the one blessing to emerge from a partnership that should never have formed. Katie was a miracle baby, born to a mother who had been permanently physically injured from years of early sexual abuse and a father consumed by his addiction.

After my daughter's birth, I fell into a cavernous depression that I could not find my way out of. I was in a psychic freefall. I remember looking into Katie's big, brown Bambi eyes and telling her that I was so sorry she got stuck with me as a mommy. Every time I held her, I found myself tearfully apologizing for not being good enough for her. As I rocked her in her baby carrier to soothe her colicky wails, I would repeat, 'I'm sorry, sweetie' over and over again. As she cried in pain, I cried in despair.

My husband, the healthcare professional, was battling his own demons and neither noticed nor cared about the suffering in his midst. In desperation, I turned to my daughter's pediatrician.

He said it sounded like postpartum depression and he referred me to a psychotherapist.

At first, I resisted his recommendation. I knew what delving into my past and my psyche would lay bare. But I was losing everything. My marriage was in shambles and there was a tiny, helpless person who looked up at me with total need. If I didn't come through for Katie, she would become me in 30 years. Therapy wasn't about me. It was about saving my daughter. The choice to undergo treatment was a supreme act of motherly love. It certainly wasn't an act of self-love.

*

My relationship with Sue, the psychotherapist, was not your typical client–therapist relationship. It started out fairly traditional, but then morphed into a tangled, intense, dual relationship. Sue and I had two incompatible ties.

There was our relationship in her basement office, where for the first time I made efforts to tentatively unburden myself. I had been mute about my torture for three decades, but in the safety of her office I reached out, desperate for solace. Miraculously, she reached back. Sometimes during therapy I would lie, curled up on her couch with my head in her lap, sobbing in anguish over a childhood memory or a current life trauma. Sue would stroke my hair, tell me she loved me, and promise me she could make it better. I clung to her every word.

In contrast, there was our relationship at the dining room table, which started after Joe and I separated. The combination of his prescription drug addiction and my emotional unraveling was more than our marriage could bear. As a result, Katie (a toddler at the time) and I became regulars at Sue's for Sunday meals, holidays, birthdays, and gatherings with her extended family. Sue's clan adopted me and Katie as loved members. The group of us took summer vacations together to Sea World, Rehoboth Beach, and all the amusement park hotspots along the east coast. I looked forward to the weekly

Trivial Pursuit game night with the adults of her family. I babysat Sue's children and she cared for Katie. We conspired together to plan her sister's surprise 40th birthday party and her mother's surprise 80th. Sue became my best friend, my cohort in crime, my mother … and my therapist.

I lived with these two relationships compartmentalized in my mind for four years. On one side of the divide dwelled the most violated and fragile parts of me. Whether I was struggling to verbalize brutal childhood experiences, sinking into suicidal depressions, or twirling around her office in frenetic and chaotic episodes – chasing evil alternate dimensional forces – I was fragile and exposed to her. On the other side of the divide, I was an integral part of her loving family.

I had never known such a thing before, and I lapped it up. Katie called Sue, "Aunty Sue". She called Sue's mom "Grandma". Sue's husband and I shared a fondness for bad disaster movies and enjoyed satirizing sappy television programs. We managed to have a lot of fun together, annoying Sue as we spoofed some syrupy movie she happened to be watching. I remember she banished us to the kitchen peevishly during one such improvisation. He and I responded by returning to the scene of the crime and parading through the living room as the tearjerker played on.

I now had people in my life who didn't hurt me. I was wanted and loved. There was no way I was ever going to risk losing this gift. I was sure Sue and her family were my reward for my years trapped in my childhood Egypt. If I could have taken up permanent residence in their guest room, I'd have done so gleefully. However, I was also severely ill with wildly out-of-control mood swings. I was eaten alive by vicious childhood memories. I needed solid mental healthcare more than I needed a mommy. I didn't understand this, but Sue should have.

For the first three years of our complex relationship, Sue told me I didn't need psychiatric treatment for my mood swings and treated my severe trauma symptoms using hypnotic regression. She hoped that by taking me back in time to the original traumas, I could express and conquer them. Repeatedly reliving those memories decimated my ability to function as an adult. I'd sit on the floor in my living room night after night, rocking, sobbing, and clutching a stuffed bunny. I didn't even know how old I was at times like that, even as Katie pleaded for my attention.

But I loved Sue. I trusted her, and I wasn't going to question her and risk losing my home. This dual relationship was untenable, but I wanted to be part of a loving family so badly that I was willing to endure inadequate mental healthcare and the absence of therapeutic boundaries. As a result, I disintegrated into a chaotic, sometimes psychotic, mess. It was only a matter of time before our artificial construct would collapse.

The festering wound that my relationship with Sue created ruptured one horrible spring afternoon in 1994. My laboratory director, who was also a dear friend of mine, called me into his office and said as gently as he could, 'We are placing you on medical leave. You need to get help.'

I stared at him blankly. I had known David for seven years, ever since he'd hired me from graduate school in 1988. He was brilliant, with a twisted sense of humor that matched my own. He was also the best boss I ever had and most likely will ever have. He was 100% Irish, 100% Chicago, and he had a lot of dynamite in his 5ft 4in frame. He took me under his professional wing and nurtured my infant career. We'd covered for each other professionally and supported each other personally.

When his wife of many years – who he adored – left him with no hint, I was the one he confided in at work. When I had a potentially career-ending conflict with corporate hierarchy, he championed my position ... and I was promoted. When he left our Fortune 500 company to take a position at a start-up laboratory chain, he took me with him. David was an anchor in my life, and this rebuke seemed to come out of nowhere.

He tried to soften the blow by adding, 'Tova, you are a gifted QA Director and a dear friend. When you have done some healing, you will always have a position here.'

I was witnessing the destruction of my carefully built professional career. It turned out that everyone I had responsibility over as a senior director knew about the demons that tormented me. Maybe, I thought, it was because of the time I danced on the chairs in the lunchroom and started a food fight (I was just having a bit of fun). Or maybe, I thought, it was because of that time the regional QA Director came for an unannounced audit and found me huddled on the floor in the corner of my office, rocking and sobbing hysterically (she should have knocked). Maybe, I thought, it was because I would tell my staff that there were malevolent forces from another universe conspiring to destroy our laboratory data and we needed to take special precautions (I was just doing my job). Whichever incident it was that motivated him to – as I saw it – unjustly take this action, I now stood before my executive laboratory director psychologically stripped and jobless.

But the day didn't end there; it just got worse. I drove to Sue's house, still reeling from my director's devastating rebuke. I couldn't wrap my head around the fact that I had no job to go to. How was that even possible? I had held down some kind of job since I was 15, when I worked in a pen clip factory after school. Suddenly it dawned on me that I had nothing to do the next day and every day after that.

I sat down in Sue's living room, trying to take stock of my lab director's words. I waited for her to come up from her basement office. It suddenly struck me as strange that her living room looked exactly the same as it did when I was there the previous weekend for dinner.

There were her family photos, which were professionally displayed on Cherrywood table surfaces. There were selected pieces of fine art hanging on her walls, which were wallpapered in royal blue and silver.

She had a tan-tooled leather couch I would often melt into while watching a movie or television program with her and her husband. My favorite view from her couch was of the sunroom, which they had filled with a trove of children's toys for Katie.

Yep, everything looked the same … but it wasn't. The person I most respected had just told me that I was too crazy to work.

Sue came into the living room to greet me. She was a truly stunning woman. She had gorgeous long chestnut tresses, green eyes, and the kind of grace only women who know they are beautiful possess.

In her office, I tried to settle into our familiar routine of talking about mutual friends, her family, and upcoming plans. Little did I know that this would be the last time Sue and I would ever speak. I suspect she knew, however. Instead of being her nurturing self, I found her uncharacteristically businesslike and jarring.

In that fragile moment, I could not afford to be rocked. I was disoriented and bereft. I needed mommy, but she was not mommy.

For over three years, Sue had struggled to contain my psychological disintegration, and at the beginning of that year she'd reluctantly referred me to a psychiatrist, Dr. Q, for help.

Dr. Q was an enigmatic figure. At our first appointment, I'd sat in his office waiting room, loathing him before I'd ever met him. I was neither cooperative nor civil to him. However, I desperately needed him. Looking back on my relationship with Dr. Q, I realized that I'd ruined the last chance I had to escape total psychiatric collapse. I was so angry at Sue and so conflicted about our dual relationship that the complexity of a third party in our drama was more than I could take in. From my perspective, this unholy alliance between him and Sue was more like collusion than collaboration, and I was not going to cooperate.

When I was finally ushered into his office, I sat across from him, glaring and studying him. I was looking for reasons to reject anything he might have to say, so of course I found them.

He was a tall man, with perfectly styled blond hair and manicured nails. He wore a tailored suit, monogrammed shirt, and gold cufflinks. I scoffed at his Brooks Brothers advertisement appearance. As I scowled at him at our first appointment, he stared imperiously back at me. Clearly, he could sense I wasn't going to engage in spontaneous disclosure, so he began asking me a series of direct questions. He asked me about my sleep patterns, energy levels, episodes of crying or elation, etc. He looked at me, expressionless, as I answered his questions in one and two-word utterances.

This interrogation seemed to go on forever. When the grilling was over, he declared himself an expert on me. He told me I had bipolar I disorder and prescribed me several medications, including lithium. I remember thinking that there was no way I was going to agree to take medications from him. But after some internal debate, I relented, filled the prescription, and took the medication. I hated giving him that victory, but my life was a mess. How could medications make it any messier?

I'd had no real experience with psychiatrists except for when, as a child, I prayed desperately that one would magically appear and make my many caregivers vanish. I had heard the grown-ups talk about psychiatrists. I ran with the fantasy that one was on the way. The fact that this unicorn MD never appeared made me both hate the entire profession before I ever met a single practitioner and yearn to become one.

The truth was, however, that I needed Dr. Q to have some awareness that besides the bipolar disorder, mine and Sue's relationship was a significant part of my problem. I wanted him to ask why someone who had been in treatment with the same psychotherapist five days a week for four years still remained seriously ill – and yet had never been referred to a psychiatrist until this point for evaluation. I also needed him to ask me about my relationship with Sue, so that I could tell him everything.

But he never asked these critical questions. Maybe he thought, 'Why bother? She isn't going to answer.' Had he asked me, however, in a tone that was inviting, I believe that I would have spilled my guts. I desperately needed an ally, but the questions were never asked. The trajectory for the next 25 years of my life was set.

I completely believed that there was a collusion between Sue and Dr. Q. This culminated in Sue, on the day that I lost my job, coldly announcing that I was being referred for inpatient care at a psychiatric hospital in a different state. She told me the facility was expert in treating severe trauma. In hindsight, this clinical decision was four years too late to salvage my sanity.

Instead of seeing the hospital admission as an opportunity, I was furious. All of a sudden, Sue had decided to get dramatically and invasively clinical in my life. All I could hear was that I was being banished by her, and by extension, Dr. Q.

She said, 'Tova, you can't take care of yourself. How do you expect to care for a three-year-old? I've arranged for Betty to care for her while you are gone.'

Joe, my ex-husband and Katie's father, was still struggling with his inner monsters. As a result, he had withdrawn completely from fatherhood. Katie only saw him sporadically and for brief periods of time. He definitely didn't have the capacity to look after Katie in my long-term absence. I knew that Betty was capable; she was both a friend and a client of Sue's and a friend of mine. Sue had introduced the two of us to one another, and we'd hit it off quickly. Katie loved Betty as an adopted aunt who gave her toys and treated her to ice cream for dinner. Betty often cared for Katie when I had to travel for work.

Sue assured me that Betty was delighted to have Katie as a guest once again. The arrangements were all set, I was told. In total shock, I slurred the words, 'But I haven't told Katie I'm leaving. I have to see her, please.'

Sue said flatly, 'No, it will only confuse her. We'll tell her everything.'

I don't recall crying or having any kind of emotional outburst at that point. It felt as though Sue had just sentenced me to death. Why didn't I just ignore her and head straight to Katie's preschool? That is a question that haunts me to this day. But I was at the nadir of my life. Good decisions were in short supply.

Sue said something about the hospital expecting me the following day and asked if I needed help making flight arrangements. I left her office, saying, 'No thanks. I think I can still dial a phone.'

Between leaving Sue's office and showing up at the hospital's admissions office the next day, I remember slowly swallowing an entire bottle of lithium tablets almost gleefully. I took perverse pleasure in the notion that I could die while in the hospital, and no one would know from what. After swallowing the lithium, I dutifully took a cab to the airport, flew to the next state on a one-way ticket, and took a cab to the hospital. I assumed it was only a matter of time before the lithium would become a problem. I never actually thought I would get caught.

I sat meekly and politely through the admissions process. I smiled at the appropriate times and bantered with the resident. Then he said, 'I see you have manic depression and are on lithium. Let's check your levels before I admit you.' That was when I panicked.

I tried to wiggle out of the lithium draw, but the resident was having none of it. I knew I was in for a bit of a wait, so I got comfortable in the dormitory-style patient short-stay room, where I was told to relax until the blood work came back. As I awaited the impending verdict, the overdose hit me. I became violently ill but kept silent.

Fooling myself, I thought maybe the resident wouldn't notice, but of course he did. Dashing into my room, he told me my lithium levels were dangerously toxic and he had called an ambulance. This was a psychiatric hospital after all, not an acute care facility, so I had to be medically treated elsewhere. This was definitely not the outcome I had fantasized about.

Was my act one of revenge or despondency? To this day, I have no idea.

I was admitted to a regional acute care hospital, where I became critically ill. I was there for maybe eight or nine days.

Upon readmission to the psychiatric hospital, I was completely off lithium and fell into the grips of a brutal psychotic–manic episode. I was placed in the hospital's "special care unit" for intensive treatment. The special care unit was designed specifically to handle patients in the midst of psychotic episodes.

I missed my daughter's fourth birthday while on that unit. I wasn't even allowed to send her a card. I remember screaming Katie's name, pounding my head against the wall, and sliding to the floor, shrieking hysterically. My anguish went unaddressed.

I have few clear memories of what I said or did during that month of confinement. It was all jumbled together in my mind – the loss of Katie, the extreme mania, and the parade of childhood tormentors that crashed through my consciousness and hounded me day and night. Reality became obliterated.

Although I later tried to enquire as to what I did during this time, staff members felt no responsibility to fill in the gaps for me. Instead, I got the diagnostic description straight out of the DSM IV, the bible of psychiatric diagnoses.

In reality, it was probably best that I wasn't privy to all the details of my behaviors while psychotic. I had endured enough shame.

Once the psychosis and mania resolved, the hospital staff transferred me to the trauma treatment floor, where I was originally supposed to be admitted before the lithium intruded. What I didn't know was that while I was in the hospital recovering from the lithium overdose, Sue had called the psychiatric facility and told them she was no longer treating me. She told them she was taking no questions and if they needed clinical information, they could contact Dr. Q.

I needed to be extricated from my relationship with her, but to have it imposed on me with such brute force was the worst kind of cruelty. The timing of Sue's decision was expedient but cowardly. There was so much she and I had to untangle, but instead I was abandoned to the care of total strangers many miles from home. I wondered what she had told her husband, her children, her mom, her sisters, her extended family. Did she reveal the innermost secrets I had confided in her? Did she make up a story about me that was convenient for her? How did Sue make me disappear from her life?

When my new therapist informed me that Sue had severed all therapeutic and personal ties with me, I listened stoically. But inside, I screamed in pain as if a limb had been severed from my body. As a result, over time, I crumbled into a functionless heap. There was nothing left of my life, fragile though it had always been. Katie was ripped away from me. My job was taken away from me. My marriage had dissolved. My self-respect and dignity had been eviscerated. Sue, my surrogate mother, had dumped me like I was garbage to be hauled away to a refuse pile. It no longer mattered to me what I did or how I behaved.

So I behaved horribly: I refused medication, wouldn't participate in groups, and refused to cooperate with any staff. Since Sue wasn't there for me to work through my grief with her, I saved my feelings of betrayal and despondency for my new inpatient therapist. I was uncooperative, combative, destructive, and ultimately incapable of helping myself. I often remained curled up in a fetal position on the floor for long periods of time. I was either lashing out or regressing into helplessness. The hospital handled my disintegration by slowly taking control over my life decisions. The more decisions they took from me, the less life I had in me, and the more I regressed.

I was kept at the psychiatric facility for eight months. In October of 1994, I was released from long-term institutional care. When I was finally discharged, stable but destroyed, I was no longer Tova, mother of Katie and QA Director for a large laboratory chain. I was now just a chronic psychiatric patient with no past and no future.

*

I was discharged with the requirement that I be admitted to a community partial hospital program. I obviously wasn't allowed to parent Katie. I had been psychologically and pharmaceutically reduced to a step just above zombie on the functioning scale. So, I sat. I rotted. My life slipped past me. Katie's life slipped past me. At this point, the conversation among the psychiatrists, social workers, and treatment staff about my future included phrases like "state hospital", "group home", and "loss of permanent custody of Katie". I had long since stopped caring what the powers that controlled my life did to me. I had given up believing that I had any future at all.

One day, in the winter of 1995, my social worker at the program said to me, 'Tova, you need a private therapist. I know you can do better than you are doing and we just can't do that level of therapy here in this program.'

I thought about my social worker's diagnosis and decided to contact Dr. Q for a referral. He had terminated our relationship not long after I started at the partial hospital program. The reason he gave was that since I was no longer in treatment with Sue, he could no longer treat me. As I saw it, he abandoned me because I was no longer in a toxic dual relationship with my ex-therapist. He truly had no idea what had really happened between me and Sue, and I wondered what exactly Sue had told him about us. The possibilities were horrifying to contemplate.

I buried my head in my hands and wept. I had no ally. Maybe, I thought, if I were seeing another therapist, he'd take me back? It wasn't that I wanted Dr. Q. It was simply that I wanted to undo the abandonment.

In my call to him, he reasserted that he wouldn't take me back as a patient because he felt a professional obligation to Sue. Clearly, he felt no such obligation to me. I choked up on the phone with him, holding back sobs. He did say I needed a highly experienced trauma psychotherapist. He recommended a woman named Carrie and assured me that she was one of the top psychologists in the city for the treatment of trauma. We hung up, having nothing more to say to each other. In my social worker's office, under her supportive eye, I made – and, surprising myself, kept – the appointment.

It was while under Carrie's care that my journey with Dr. Guterson began.

CHAPTER 2

Trust me

HE'S ONE OF THE GOOD ONES

I took inventory of the waiting room in Carrie's office, which was more akin to a wide hallway than an actual room. People wandered in and out. Some took up residence in the cloth-seated, straight-backed chairs that lined the windowless wall. Several therapists used this waiting area, and unfortunately, not all their offices were soundproof. I tried to avoid being a silent witness to some stranger's therapy session by occupying myself with the paintings on the walls.

There was one painting in particular that grabbed my attention. It was a Victorian era portrait of a young mother combing the hair of her grimacing little daughter. The child was resistant and the mother looked determined. I thought maybe the painting was a metaphor for the therapeutic process, or at least a metaphor for my therapeutic process. As I continued to entertain myself with this line of thought, a middle-aged petite blonde emerged from of one of the offices. *Thank goodness, it's one of the silent offices,* I thought to myself. She glanced at the row of people sitting in the waiting area and quietly asked for me by my first name. As I rose, she greeted me with a smile and ushered me into her office.

I was immediately intrigued by her voice. Carrie had the most delicate cadence I had ever heard. I thought, *bet she's good at soothing fussy babies.* Her office was comfortable and not at all ostentatious. She liked plants, but there were no photos or any hint of anything personal about her in the room. After years with Sue, I was profoundly grateful for the anonymity. It was a pretty safe assumption that a therapist who chose not to display personal aspects of her life wasn't going to invite me home with her for dinner. Still, I remained inconsolable with grief from Sue's abandonment. A trusting relationship with another psychotherapist seemed almost an impossibility. I sunk into Carrie's plush, pillow-laden paisley couch. She offered me tea, and I mused that all therapists should serve tea. There is something incredibly humanizing and civilizing about the steeped beverage.

As I sipped my brew and waited for the session to begin, my thoughts drifted toward my current circumstance. What did I want this new person to know about me? What was safe to share with her? What should I keep to myself? As I pondered my plight, I felt only resignation. I was sure that this relationship was doomed to fail before it even started. I was presenting myself to this new therapist as a thing that had been physically and emotionally stripped of most of what had made her human. The system that was supposed to help me had murdered me. The previous five years of my life had been top heavy in "mental health experts" yet devoid of real help. I didn't even know why I was at that appointment, except that my social worker had gone to a lot of trouble to encourage me to arrange it. It would have been impolite for me to not show up.

But the question was, would I come back? A lot depended on whether this latest therapist could work miracles, and I wasn't counting on it. I was a hardened veteran: cynical, suspicious, devoid of hope, and way over-medicated. The partial hospital program, my year of inpatient captivity, and the Sue and Dr. Q regime: each experience taught me how to endure shame and indifference.

A very stark example of how I had morphed into someone unrecognizable was that in 1994, just before my hospital confinement, I'd weighed 132 pounds. As I sat in Carrie's office that day, I weighed 267 pounds. That was how little I cared about myself. It wasn't that I was incapable of more. It was that I had been stripped of the belief that I was capable of more. So, as my essence was destroyed, I filled the emptiness up with the trappings of being chronically mentally ill.

Looking back at this time in my life, I have come to understand that my illnesses became not simply an aspect of me, but all that I had left of me.

So I took on the identity of a sick person. In a way, taking up the role of "psychiatric patient" absolved most of life's pesky obligations. The people in your life come to not expect much from you, and it's easy to deliver on that expectation. Not that I had many friends left from my pre-hospitalization years. They had all drifted away, pitying me. I only had my new, partial hospital friends. My worldview became myopic. My new "friends" were all mentally ill and in the same day program I was in. We bonded out of necessity. People shared the details of their illnesses and hospitalizations. They'd critique staff based on how kind and attentive they were to patients. They affirmed for each other the reasons they were too sick to do any given task. People shared misinformation about medications and complained about side effects, real or imagined.

The worst, however, was the "I'm sicker than you are" game. If someone had a symptom, someone else would have a worse one. If someone were in crisis, the next day three people would be in crisis. It was a competition straight to the bottom.

For the most part, I was a chronicler of these behaviors rather than a participant. However, I was not completely immune to the allure of getting staff attention. My least attractive behavior occurred when someone, staff or patient, said something to me that brought back a painful childhood memory. I'd sit in front of the staff lounge door weeping and rocking, desperate for comfort. I rarely got it.

In addition, I became everyone's confidante. I heard all about who slighted who, who resented who, who thought who wasn't really "sick enough" to be in treatment. Five years earlier, I'd been a mother, a respected scientist, well educated, a returned Peace Corps volunteer, an amateur World War One historian, and financially independent. Now I was spending my days gossiping with other psychiatric patients, all of us living off disability and trying to meet such unambitious goals as brushing our teeth or making our beds.

My life during this time revolved around the partial hospital program I attended five days a week, six hours a day, and the 1970s television programs I watched at night. The hospital days were filled up with a haphazardly arranged schedule of "groups". There was goals group, journaling group, group therapy, "ask the nurse" group, arts and crafts, recreation group, and lunch. Dotted among these groups were check-in appointments with my assigned social worker and medication appointments with whichever medical resident happened to be on rotation that month. The physicians were a dizzying parade of faces, and the staff had a high turnover.

The most vexing problem was that the people there to guide us through our illnesses were themselves worn down and jaded. Chronically mentally ill people need a lot of time, attention, and compassion. What brought out the worst in patients was a belief that if they could just get the staff's attention, their torment would be cared about and addressed. However, most of the staff were too preoccupied with holding back chaos to see the desperation behind all the acting-out behaviors.

After a long day of "care", I would return home to a messy house, empty pizza boxes, and endless hours of 1970s television reruns, particularly *M*A*S*H*. I didn't read anymore. I was, in my previous life, a current events fanatic. I literally could rattle off the names of every Justice on the Supreme Court and their major decisions. Suddenly, there were days when I wasn't even sure who the president was. I had bought into the lie that I could not be healed and believed this new reality was as good as life was going to get for me. The talk of a state hospital admission no longer seemed all that awful.

And somehow, I was now supposed to communicate all of this to Carrie, the total stranger sitting in front of me. That depth of disclosure would take time and trust. I had the time, but I lacked the ability to trust. Again, I knew any chance at a relationship with her was hopeless.

Yet, something kept me nestled among the pillows on her couch. I sat there with so much baggage weighing me down, and I just couldn't carry it anymore. At least, I couldn't carry it alone. I needed anything this woman could pass on to me. So, I stayed on the couch. Because, did I really have anything left to lose?

Carrie and I spent that first session rather uneventfully going over history, signing medical and psychotherapy releases, and discussing my current therapeutic arrangement. Over the next months, Carrie – unlike with any other therapist I had had in the past – was willing to help me explore the abuses I had suffered while undergoing "treatment". As I slowly shared my traumatic journey with her, Carrie was genuinely outraged by what I had lived through. She used the words "ethics violations", "boundary violations", and "cruelty".

I was taken aback by how aghast she was at my care. No one, that I could remember, had ever taken my suffering seriously. Carrie was so horrified by my experiences that she felt the need to verify my story. She wanted to be certain I was being factual and not delusional in my retelling of events. She called Sue. When I next saw Carrie, she told me Sue shocked her by both admitting to the details of her grossly inappropriate behavior and asserting that she had encouraged the bizarre relationship as therapy. Sue had had the gall to tell Carrie that she was willing to "take me back" if I had "learned my lesson".

Carrie was dumbfounded. She also had all the proof she needed to move forward with my healing.

For the first time, I felt protected and safe in therapy. So, when she asked me that standard, trite, therapist question, 'What are your goals for treatment?', I had an honest answer. I told her that I wanted to be Katie's mom again. Carrie looked at me and with complete confidence told me that yes, I would be Katie's mom again. My eyes welled up with tears and I spontaneously hugged her, a rare gesture for me. This was the type of therapy I needed. Our singular goal now was getting mommy and daughter back together again. To make that happen, I had to let Carrie deconstruct my current life and build the framework for a future one. We didn't do much trauma work. Carrie and I knew that I wasn't ready. Instead, we set out to reconstruct my life with Katie at the center.

At that point, Katie was in her father's care, as my ex-husband had resurfaced in her life during my long confinement. I saw her whenever he would let me. The visits were heart-wrenching for me and Katie. Every separation felt like a fresh loss for my sweet five-year-old. It killed me to see her grief and I hated myself all the more for being its source.

It didn't help that my ex-husband struggled with his role as a full-time single father. He would often rely on a stable of different people to babysit for him. The sickening reality that my baby girl had multiple caretakers, just as I had, ripped at my gut. Her little life was in chaos and I had no way of knowing if she was even safe. I finally had to acknowledge that my gentle daughter really did need me, and that I didn't have the luxury of abandoning sanity without a fight.

That insight was my very first therapeutic breakthrough, and, much to my utter shock, that miracle I had once snickered at seemed to be materializing.

My treatment regimen now consisted of the partial hospital program, where I also received care from the random psychiatrists who would drift through, and private therapy with Carrie. I was content with this arrangement. Content, that is, until one deeply shaming encounter with a program psychiatrist, which set me on a journey that has now entered its 20th year.

In October 1995, I had my typical medication appointment with whoever the psychiatrist was that month. This time it was Dr. X. I shuffled into his borrowed office and sat down. The room was a nondescript box. It was cramped, windowless, and chilly. Dr. X sat behind a metal desk and I sat in a metal chair. He was a young man, short, with a thick Indian accent that I struggled to understand.

He had a surprise for me. He told me that a group of new psychiatry residents were studying trauma patients and he'd like to know if I would be willing to answer some of their questions. I thought about it, and I decided that given how poorly trauma is understood by psychiatrists, I liked the idea of maybe educating a few baby docs. I told Dr. X that I would do it. He said he'd get back to me. So, I left the office feeling like I might have some speck of value left after all.

A couple of hours later, Dr. X pulled me out of a group and said he needed to speak to me. I followed him into a different nondescript and frigid office. I sat down. He continued to stand, peering down at me in disgust. In a contemptuous voice, he snarled, 'You are a liar and a manipulator.' He hissed that no one who has ever had real trauma would ever consent to share that experience with total strangers. In a voice dripping with derision, he revealed that the story about the psychiatric residents was a "test" to see if my trauma experiences were real.

He finished his execution of me by declaring, 'You failed the test.' He turned on his heel and strode out of the room. I sat alone in that office, frozen. I didn't know Dr. X. I'd never had any kind of conversation with him. I didn't recall ever behaving in a way that would generate that kind of cruelty from him. The blows came from nowhere and from this total stranger. There was nothing I could emotionally or cognitively latch onto that made sense of what this MD had just done to me. I kept repeating to myself, 'What did I do? What did I do wrong? I don't understand.'

I left the program in the middle of the day. I was acting on pure survival instinct, like an amoeba reflexively avoiding the pain of a probe. I called Carrie, barely able to speak between heaving sobs. It wasn't my appointment day but she made room for me. In her office, I curled up in a tiny ball on the floor, hysterically shaking and gasping, and I began reliving a brutal trauma from kindergarten.

The full weight of his corpulent body pinned my five-year-old frame to the twin bed that I was trying desperately to dissolve into.

'I own you,' he hissed. 'Do you know that? You are bought and paid for. That house you live in? That car you ride in? The food on your plate? I paid for all of it in exchange for YOU. You will do exactly what I want you to do, or else you and everyone else you know will have NOTHING.'

The sudden realization that everyone in my world would starve if I didn't obey the Snake sucked the air out of my lungs. I scrunched my eyes shut, bracing myself for the Snake to enter. I listened to a train as it passed by the little Cape Cod cottage that he lived in. I screamed in my head to the train, 'Don't leave without me! Wherever you are going, take me with you!'

I imagined faraway places where there were no snakes: Providence, RI; Bangor, Maine; even Montreal, Canada. I imagined grand adventures that took me far away from what was about to happen. When the Snake deposited himself, the hiss turned to excited utterances.

'Swallow, Tova, swallow now!' he panted.

I pleaded with myself. It's chocolate milk. It's just chocolate milk. You can swallow that.

In one hard gulp, the "chocolate milk" went down. He dismounted me and, smug with satisfaction, said, 'Get some sleep.'

I rolled over in the bed and vomited the "chocolate milk" all over the hardwood floor. Terrified, I ordered myself, 'Clean this up or there might be more "chocolate milk" tonight.' I sopped up my own vomit with a bathroom towel and threw the towel into the garbage. Sleep seemed like a silly grown-up order to get little girls to forget snakes.

I was trapped in this 1965 memory, and on my own could not get back to 1995. I don't know what Carrie did to bring me back to the present and soothe me enough for conversation, but when my sobs subsided to sniffles, she gave me a gentle reality check. Carrie reminded me that my trauma history was well documented and was all too real. It occurred to me that Dr. X had never bothered to look at my medical history before he pronounced me lower than pond scum. I stopped shaking. Then Carrie said the words that would chart a brand-new course for my life. She said I needed a private psychiatrist.

The following day was my regularly scheduled appointment. I was a bit more glued together but still badly shaken. She said, 'I have a private psychiatrist I want you to see.' I panicked and told her I was never seeing another psychiatrist, ever.

'Dr. Q was a disaster! Dr. X was a disaster! Why should this new person be any better?' I shouted at her. I don't think I stomped my feet, but I was close.

Then, in an assertive but reassuring tone, she said, 'Trust me, Tova, he's one of the good ones.' Carrie told me he had just finished his residency. She knew him from her work at the major psychiatric hospital in our city. He was setting up his private practice and she believed he and I would be a good clinical fit. She handed me a card with his name, office phone number, and office address, and made me promise that I would make an appointment. After much tortured indecision, I made the call and, on a snowy afternoon in November, Dr. Guterson and I met for the first time. My brutalized psyche was about to meet the most powerful ally she had ever experienced, an ally she still relies on today.

*

I sat in the small waiting room of an office in the medical arts building of a local hospital. It seemed to me that I was always sitting in some room waiting for some psychiatrist, therapist, social worker, mental health aid, etc. I kept coming up with elaborate reasons to escape impending doom. Maybe I could say my dog died (I didn't have a dog). Maybe I could say I had spontaneously recovered and therefore didn't need his services (not likely to be believed). Maybe I could tell him I had a scheduling conflict that would last at least a year (wasn't I emigrating to Israel soon?). I kept myself entertained coming up with fanciful ways to escape this appointment.

As I got up to dash out the door, Carrie's words came to mind. 'Trust me, Tova, he's one of the good ones.' I *did* trust Carrie, so I sat back down and continued to wait, wishing still that I had a dog.

Dr. Yaakov Guterson stepped out of his office and into the waiting room. He greeted me warmly. I sized him up. He was tall, had a dark beard, wore a yarmulke and glasses, and was casually dressed. He actually looked like how I always imagined a psychiatrist should appear. He had that classic young Sigmund Freud look about him. His smile seemed genuine and his voice was warm and welcoming. I was intrigued by him and thought, *I can at least try to talk to this guy.* So I meekly followed him into his office and took a seat.

It took every ounce of energy and concentration I had just to keep myself in the chair. The specter of Dr. X and Dr. Q loomed large in Dr. Guterson's office. I kept telling myself: *don't talk too much about your complicated trauma history. He might not believe you. Don't tell him about the psychotic mania episode from your inpatient odyssey. He might think you're too much of a problem. Finally, whatever you do, don't tell him about Dr. X. He's going to take the word of another psychiatrist over a crazy person.*

Then I started to panic that maybe he already knew about Dr. X and he already knew about my complex trauma history. Maybe he already knew about the bipolar disorder and psychosis. I thought maybe he knew all of it and he was like Dr. X, setting up a trap in order to humiliate me. All I was certain of was that the list of forbidden topics was extensive and I was suspicious of him to the point of being paranoid.

So, what did we talk about on that first day? I detailed the barest of essential information, leaving out huge chunks of critical clinical facts. He asked me how I spent my day. I told him about the partial hospital program, talk radio, and *M*A*S*H* reruns. Most importantly, he asked about my history. *The life I had when I was actually a human being,* I thought to myself. I lit up at the opportunity to talk about Katie, Peace Corps, grad school, my science career, and my travels to East Africa, Israel, and the UK. I found myself starting to relax a bit and warm up to him. I think I even laughed at one point. He was gentle, engaging, and soft-spoken. I scoured his every word and vocal inflection for ridicule, yet could find nothing threatening. I needed a lot more data, but at that moment, I wasn't afraid of him. Another breakthrough.

We moved on to talk about my medications. The list of drugs that I was taking at the time looked more like a pharmacy formulary than what actually should be found in someone's medicine cabinet. Although I was embarrassed, he didn't judge me. Instead, he said that we would work on simplifying my medication regimen.

I specifically remember him targeting the Klonopin. He said that was the first drug he'd like to see me come off of. 'Tova, life is full of anxiety. It's better to learn to handle it than medicate it,' he said.

I looked at him, astonished. I had always hated taking Klonopin. The inpatient hospital had put me on it after my manic episode and the drug had just never gone away. I knew it had the potential to be addictive and, although I had no addiction history, the drug still scared me. I had enough issues. I didn't need to be addicted to a prescription drug on top of them, but I didn't know who I could tell.

Well, Dr. Guterson beat me to it. I was almost sold on this guy as my psychiatrist.

Just as I was preparing to leave, Dr. Guterson said something to me that became the cornerstone of what would be our enduring relationship. He said, 'I believe in your ability to heal, Tova.'

And you know what? At that moment, I believed that he believed that. I didn't believe it, but I was willing to let him hold on to my hope for safekeeping. So not only did I return for the next appointment, but also for every appointment after that.

Our doctor-patient journey had begun.

CHAPTER 3

Getting to know you

In that first session, Dr. Guterson planted in my tortured mind the seeds of possibility. He saw potential in me that I couldn't see myself. I walked away from our appointment daring to entertain even the remotest possibility that the state hospital wasn't my destiny.

However, throwing my lot in with his was an extremely risky move for me. He was already starting with two huge deficits. He was a guy and he was a physician. The brutality of my childhood had left me wary and self-protective about men. Also, I came into the relationship having 35 years of experience as a traumatized child, whose wounds were treated but whose pleas for safety had gone unheeded. This trust thing would be a long time coming between the two of us.

I couldn't help but ask myself why I thought Dr. Guterson would respond any differently to my anguish than all those MDs that preceded him. And every time I did, I answered myself with Carrie's words: 'He's one of the good ones.'

From Dr. X to the first ER physician who'd ever treated my childhood injuries, I found compassion to be a scarce resource in the medical profession. Yet here I was, once again, contemplating putting my sanity, safety, and Katie's future in the hands of yet another MD. I was desperate to avoid another abandonment by someone professing to be "helping" me. I knew I could not endure one more blow from a "professional".

From this first principle was born the "Tova Doctrine". I was certain that if I focused every word I uttered and every action I took through the lens of avoiding abandonment, Dr. Guterson just might work out.

The rules of engagement under which I chose to operate with him were stringent. I imposed a strict information blackout on my complex trauma history and my troubled encounters with the mental health establishment. I decided I would only reveal details of the terrible psychiatric symptoms I needed relief from when there was a crisis to manage. If I obeyed the rules, I was certain Dr. Guterson would never become Dr. X or Dr. Q. He would never call me a liar or choose a professional relationship over my care.

The problem with these laws was that they left little room for actually treating what I walked into his office needing help with. I was more desperate to stave off shame and desertion than I was concerned about the consequences of hiding crucial information from my psychiatrist. All this was the crushing consequence of being a refugee from failed therapeutic relationships.

No surprise, it didn't take long for there to be a crisis. My symptoms, because of my self-imposed silence, began to swallow me up. I would drift in and out of crises and Dr. Guterson didn't know their origins. He was left trying to manage chaos in the dark.

The demons of my childhood gnawed at my gut relentlessly. At the epicenter of the struggle was this three-year-old child embedded inside my psyche, who could not grow up because she couldn't find peace. She needed to be rescued, protected, and affirmed. She thought she'd found her mommy in Sue only to once again be thrown away like trash by another adult. She would not be easily comforted or healed. Even Carrie couldn't reach her.

What I didn't understand at the time was that healing that three-year-old was at the core of Dr. Guterson's and my journey.

Until he and I established an absolute bond, that toddler's desperation would go unheeded, and I would continue to walk on the edge of sanity.

My past was destroying my present and future. I heard the menacing hisses of my tormentors' voices as I laid in bed at night, wrapped like a mummy in bedding for protection. I heard their profanity-laced ranting speaking to me from the radio. The sound of a New England accent in a total stranger's speech could reduce me to quivering jello with the first dropped "r". I saw my tormentors' faces in mirrors, windows, and on television screens. I looked into their eyes and saw illness and rage.

When I could no longer tolerate their intrusions into my reality, I railed against the grave dangers they presented, in my mind, to the entire human race. The monsters took on mythic proportions and possessed supernatural abilities. They weren't mortals to me. They were omnipotent and omniscient, and they toyed with us mere humans like a child plays with dolls. They controlled natural disasters, plane crashes, terrorist attacks, and any injurious event that happened in the lives of people I cared about. Their constant menacing would sometimes throw me deep into suicidal depressions or psychosis-induced frenzies. It may have been 1996 for Dr. Guterson, but for the toddler inside me it was always the 1960s.

There were times when the past's relentless onslaught caused me to retreat into an imaginary world where no one could reach me. I'd dwell in the world of 1960s and 70s television programs. *Little House on the Prairie, The Waltons, My Three Sons* and *The Brady Bunch* were the families of my inner world. I'd dwell in Plum Creek or Walton's Mountain, protected and cherished. Pa Ingalls and Ma Walton became my parents. Uncle Charlie was my lovable, curmudgeonly uncle.

Fantasy replaced reality in the safety of my mind, but to the external world I was motionless and vacant. I would lose hours on my couch being embedded in my inner space, not noticing the passage of time. Yet through the blur of all these psychotic, trauma-driven, depressive episodes, there was Dr. Guterson, calmly and patiently managing the crises with little data to work with.

The "Tova Doctrine" held firm even as I disintegrated.

*

Dr. Guterson is predominantly an inpatient psychiatrist with a small private practice and, as such, I benefited greatly from this mix of his skills. I needed both his expertise in intense crisis management and the calmer one-on-one interactions in his quiet office. During the first ten years of our relationship, he was Director of Psychiatry at a bustling community hospital. Through those years, I became a semi-regular guest at the facility. Memories of these early hospitalizations run together, but one admission stands out as extraordinary. It helped forge the enduring bond he and I now have.

This critical moment of connection occurred between us during one of these early admissions. In the winter of 1996, Dr. Guterson hospitalized me. I was repeatedly reliving a brutal childhood memory, the details of which I refused to share with him, even as I relived the event in vivid color, odor, and sound.

'Cuddles is DEAD. Cuddles is DEAD!!' Janet screeched from the bedroom that she and I were forced to share. I pulled myself away from my algebra homework and ran upstairs to find her running in frenzied circles, shrieking and cupping the lifeless hamster in her 11-year-old hands. Trying to soothe her, I offered to get another Cuddles for her.

Her eyes bulged, her face contorting into a freakish expression that made me back away reflexively. 'THERE IS NO OTHER CUDDLES! THE SAINTS WILL RESURRECT HIM! I JUST NEED TO PRAY THE MIRACLE WORDS OF THE SAINTS!' she screamed.

And so it began. All night, she babbled gibberish incantations to the Saints, still cupping the dead hamster. There was no sleep in that bedroom after Cuddles died.

The next morning, when her beloved hamster was still lifeless, Janet sneaked out of our caregiver's house to make the trek to a nearby religious shrine. She reappeared about midday with a container of water.

This isn't going to end well, *I thought to myself.*

Janet told me excitedly that she had the magic potion to restore her adored hamster to his lively self. She dashed up the stairs, picked up the lifeless rodent that she had carefully laid on her pillow, and immersed his body in the shrine water. The gibberish incantations began again. As day turned into night and Cuddles still refused to run on his wheel, Janet began shrieking her incantations, in between sobbing and pounding her head on the wall.

Finally, one of her caretakers took notice, and I begged to be allowed to bury Cuddles. Furious at my suggestion, the caretaker told me, 'Don't you dare lay a finger on that hamster.' Cuddles was returned to his hamster cage. Janet poured the remainder of the shrine water into it, and her hysteria continued until she collapsed of exhaustion.

When one lets a dead animal lie around long enough in a house with some flies ... the inevitable happens. The putrid odor and hamster teaming with maggots in my bedroom compelled me to act against adult instruction. In the middle of the night, I got a shoebox, picked up the maggot-laden hamster, and buried him in the backyard. I suppressed my reflex to gag as I bent over Cuddles' grave, sobbing hysterically over having to do a deed that the adults refused to do. I was 12 years old, and I had to be the grown-up.

When Janet awoke and ran to the hamster cage, she squealed with delight, 'Cuddles was resurrected!' What I didn't know then was how deeply the incident would penetrate my subconscious. Janet was free of Cuddles. I never will be.

The image of that maggot-infested dead hamster penetrated every crevasse of my consciousness. I couldn't cope with it any longer and I tried to harm myself. Dr. Guterson felt I needed to be kept safe until the episode resolved itself. In the hospital, curled up in a fetal position on the frigid linoleum floor of the "seclusion room", I retreated deep into a *Little House on the Prairie* episode for protection.

The "seclusion room" was located close to the nursing station. The room itself was stripped down to just a bed screwed to the floor, with a vinyl-covered mattress fused to the bed frame. The walls were white, made dingy by dim light and the stains of thrown food. This room was reserved for people who were either a severe threat to themselves or others. The staff had deemed me a severe threat to myself.

As usual, I had no sense of time passing as I laid motionless and unresponsive. Time in a psychiatric hospital has a way of freezing anyway, but when you are in the clutches of the past, it also regresses. Every staff member I encountered in the present became a monster from history. It was 1963 for me and I was three years old, even though for the staff and Dr. Guterson it was 1996 and I was 36 years old.

As I laid there, balled up, I was consumed by the sound of Janet's screams. The louder her voice shrieked, the deeper I crawled into myself. I ran for Pa Ingalls so that he could battle the memory for me.

The only external awareness I had was the pungent odor of disinfectant mixed with human urine. That odor permeated the entire psychiatric unit. I was overwhelmingly aware of the rancid smell to the exclusion of almost every other scent, sound, or visual image. I was encapsulated in the nearly impenetrable fortress that I had built from childhood. Very little of the external world ever penetrated my walls.

At some point, Dr. Guterson entered the room. I was made only vaguely aware of his presence by the low, soothing tenor of his voice. He was talking to me; I was listening to Pa Ingalls play the fiddle. This was not the best setting for good psychiatrist–patient communication.

Then, through my fortress, I heard him say, gently, 'I know you are having a very hard time of it right now. I promise, we will get through this.'

I had a sudden jolt of awareness. *Did he just say "we" will get through this?* Not "you" will get through this? Was he actually saying that I wasn't in this torment alone? No physician had ever included himself in my treatment.

I pulled away from the Ingalls family long enough to open one eye and peek at him. He was sitting on my bed. Stroking his dark beard and looking down at me pensively, he noticed that I was looking up at him. He smiled warmly and said confidently, 'This will get better, trust me.' In that moment, I believed him to the depths of my soul. I would have done anything he asked me to do.

A fragile bond was forged in that moment. Over time, it would only become tensile.

*

With time, medication, and Dr. Guterson's empathy, that trauma response resolved itself. I was discharged and I tried to pick up the fragmented pieces of my life. Months of treatment passed, and finally, a wondrous event materialized toward the end of 1996. I was to regain custody of Katie.

I had worked single-mindedly, during the years I was in treatment with Carrie, to bring my daughter home. When the time came to discuss Katie's return to my care, Carrie – as one of her last acts as my therapist – set up a meeting between me and my ex-husband. With a look of relief, Joe agreed to give me custody. He asked very few questions during the whole process, which surprised me, but I didn't care about his motives. All that mattered to me was my sweet little Katie was coming home.

The moment of Katie's return is etched into my consciousness, much like her hospital newborn photo and her first Purim costume.

My petite, sweet-dispositioned first-grader stood hesitantly at the base of the stairs – stairs that lead up to a brick-sided house she barely remembered was once her home. She carried a pink Hello Kitty backpack and clutched her favorite stuffed bunny.

The much adored and well-worn rabbit was in serious need of a bath, but her little lamb pajamas were still pastel green and yellow.

Katie lamented that her bunny was dirty. I gently assured her that after a quick spin in the washing machine, White Bunny would be sparkling again. She looked up at me with a kind of doubt on her little face, a doubt that I knew had more to do with me than her concern over White Bunny smudges.

I knelt down on the sidewalk so she and I were eye level with each other. Our eyes locked for a moment and she turned away. Fighting back tears, I took her little hands and promised her again that soon I would have White Bunny sparkling. Katie's face scrunched up at me as if she was pondering some deep philosophical mystery. I looked at her quizzically and she, with deadly seriousness, asked me a question that clued me in to what she was feeling.

'Can you make White Bunny smell like my sheets at daddy's house?'

I smiled at her as I held back my tears. 'Yes, sweetie,' I choked out. 'I can make White Bunny smell like your sheets at daddy's house.'

She took my hand and led me up the stairs toward our front door. As I opened the door, she burst through before me, ran upstairs to her room, and declared – as only a six-year-old girl can – 'My room needs purple sparkly curtains!'

I gave her my best serious parent face and responded, 'You are absolutely right. Purple and sparkly it is.'

She danced around the room and dove onto her bed, spread eagle, declaring, 'Hi, bed. I missed you.' Katie was indeed home.

Although I was terrified of being responsible for Katie again, I knew I had Dr. Guterson and my new therapist, Nancy, to guide me through the complex labyrinth of parenting while mentally ill.

Because of a forced change in my health insurance I had had to change therapists, so Carrie had referred me to Nancy. She was a child development expert with who I explored every aspect of my parenting for the decade I saw her. My parenting, not my trauma, became the focus of my work in therapy. I was doing everything in my power to not become the monster to my daughter that my many caretakers had been to me. Unlike the adults in my life, I was taking full advantage of the mental health services available to me. I wanted to be the best parent possible for Katie, despite my serious psychiatric illnesses.

Also, armed with Joe's health insurance, I performed a careful search to find the best child therapist available to support Katie. I signed releases so that my therapist and Dr. Guterson could speak candidly with Katie's therapist. I wanted my life to be as transparent as I could possibly make it. I wasn't threatened by the unfettered access I gave Katie's psychologist to my treatment team. To the contrary, I wanted as many therapeutic eyes as possible watching over my gentle six-year-old. I needed all the help I could get. I loved my daughter deeply and unconditionally, but I was not ignorant of the enormity of the task I was undertaking.

Katie's return infused me with life and purpose. However, there was a growing problem that pervaded every area of my daily practical existence. Where at one time I was comfortably living on a six-figure salary, I was now reduced to living on roughly a grand a month from long-term disability insurance, plus whatever child support my ex-husband decided to give me that month. We had no formal child support agreement, so the amount he chose to give was at his discretion. Medical bills had eaten up my savings over the years and I was left with only disability insurance from my former employer to support me and Katie. As I contemplated my dire financial status, I realized that after rent, food, and utilities, there wasn't much money left for things like medication.

I was too petrified of my ex-husband to ask for more child support. He made a not-so-veiled threat that if I asked for more money, he'd take custody of Katie away from me, legally. I knew that I wouldn't survive if he chose that route. As a result, I only asked for money to cover emergency expenses for Katie. My medication crisis definitely did not qualify.

I made an anonymous phone call to the local welfare office once, hoping that at least food stamps would be available. I was told I had to produce a child support agreement. I had no such agreement and abject terror prevented me from asking for one. I hung up the phone and simultaneously hung my head in shame. I never tried calling them again.

I was also too shamed by my poverty to tell Dr. Guterson about my medication pickle. I tried to solve the cash-flow problem on my own by conserving my supply of medications. I took smaller doses, skipped doses, or ignored one drug or another completely at varying intervals. In other words, I was both medication noncompliant and practicing medicine without a license. I was not taking my medications as prescribed by Dr. Guterson and, as a result, a needless, vicious cycle began: lack of adequate medication led to symptoms, and symptoms led to hospitalizations and more separations from Katie.

I don't think I ever expressed the severity of my financial crisis to anyone, least of all Dr. Guterson. He was once again in the midst of managing multiple crisis hospitalizations, and again, I deprived him of essential information that could have resulted in a resolution. I was mortified by the bedlam I was creating in everyone's lives and humiliated by my poverty. The more shame I felt, the more silent I became. I was averaging one hospitalization every six or seven months. Katie would usually stay with a close family friend, or, on a rare occasion, Joe would take her if there was no other option. She was safely cared for, but her life was being repeatedly disrupted, complicating our healing relationship.

The hospitalizations were productive, however. They stabilized me on my medications, and predictably, there was a vast improvement in my symptoms. But then I would be discharged. I couldn't pay for all my medication because my child liked to eat, and the cycle would begin all over again.

This revolving door didn't stop spinning until finally, out of sheer desperation, I confided the truth to Dr. Guterson. Avoiding his gaze, I whispered that I couldn't afford the medications he had prescribed. I explained to him that just one of my prescriptions cost $1,100 a month. I was on four different medications and facing a monthly pharmacy bill of almost $2,500. There was no way to reconcile that expense with my checking account. But Dr. Guterson and I both agreed that the drugs were quite effective when I took them appropriately. Very sensitively, he suggested I do some research on prescription assistance programs.

Through my investigations, I learned that various pharmaceutical companies had programs where I could apply for free medication. I learned about generic drugs that I could discuss taking with Dr. Guterson. I learned about alternative health insurance plans I could enroll in that had a prescription component. In addition, Dr. Guterson became quite generous with samples of my newer, more expensive drugs.

When my sources for medication became reliable, a miracle happened. My symptoms began to abate and so did the number and intensity of hospitalizations. Dr. Guterson never once expressed frustration or judgement with my long-tortured silence or my willful noncompliance. He was all about just solving the problem so that my recovery could continue.

The next obstacle I faced with medications was adjusting to them once I began taking them as prescribed. Once again, my fear of being abandoned by Dr. Guterson stopped me from giving him essential information.

I remember vividly when he prescribed me Seroquel. It is an atypical antipsychotic and he thought it might enhance the antipsychotic I was already taking. The problem with Seroquel is that it is intensely sedating. When I first began taking the drug, I felt like I was submerged in sludge. Every physical move I tried to make was slow and labored. It felt as if the air had weight when I lifted a limb. In conversation, my speech was on a time delay. Katie would ask me a question and I had to fight through the sludge to answer her. I slept 14 hours a day and when I wasn't asleep, all I thought about was being asleep.

My typical day during the early adjustment to Seroquel was arranged around being in bed as much as possible. I'd get up in the morning long enough to get Katie ready for school. I'd walk her to the bus stop, hug her, and wave goodbye as she excitedly boarded the bus in whatever sparkly dress she had chosen for herself that day. All around me were mothers in my neighborhood chatting with each other, inviting each other over for coffee, and swapping stories about their elementary school parent frustrations. I could barely get out a "good morning" to the gaggle of moms gathered at the crosswalk. I was compelled to crawl back into bed as quickly as I could before I fell face down in the middle of the crosswalk in front of these women. I'd make it to my bedroom and collapse on my bed, in my clothes, and sleep from 9am until my alarm screamed that it was time to pick up Katie from the bus stop at 4pm. As I wiped the sleep from my eyes, I would catalogue what needed to be done in the house.

I felt like a complete failure. The breakfast dishes would remain on the dining room table. The carpets would need to be vacuumed. The laundry would need to be done. Seeing the laundry, I would then fret over whether or not Katie had a clean dress to wear the next day, or if there were groceries that needed to be bought. And there always were.

Grocery shopping was overwhelming. The act of parking, navigating the shopping cart around humans and objects, roaming aisles blankly looking for Cheerios or eggs, fumbling with my checkbook while everyone behind in line glared at me, was like torture.

I tried to reserve every ounce of effort for Katie's evenings. Once the 4pm alarm blasted in my ear, I would pick her up at the bus stop and we would have a snack of apple sauce and cheese together. She would eagerly tell me about her day in very great detail. Katie never left out a single adjective and I loved to listen to her stream of consciousness monologues. I never had to say anything profound, and her full day filled my empty one.

I'd then let her watch a Disney video, usually *Aladdin*, and I'd make dinner. I was a master chef with boxed macaroni and cheese, spaghetti, and scrambled eggs. After dinner, I would help Katie with her homework and get her ready for bed. My last heroic act of the night would be reading Katie's bedtime story. There were nights that I panicked about reading to her from the latest installment of *Little House on the Prairie* or a new chapter in *Harry Potter and the Sorcerer's Stone*. I wasn't sure I could form spoken words for what was written on the page. I began to question if I even knew how to read anymore.

As soon as Katie was snuggled under her *Little Mermaid* comforter with White Bunny, I went to bed. There were nights when I slept in my clothes, too exhausted to put on my pajamas.

This pattern went on for months. Again, I was too terrified to tell Dr. Guterson. I had it in my head that either he wouldn't believe me, he wouldn't care, or he'd be angry with me. So I said nothing. I would rather sleep my life away than risk his rejection. The specters of Dr. X and Dr. Q loomed larger than ever in my relationship with him.

During this time, I noticed that there was a reoccurring theme in our conversations. Dr. Guterson would ask, very casually, 'How are you adjusting to the Seroquel?'

I would answer him in a monotone whisper, while staring at my hands, 'Fine.'

With suspicion, he'd respond, 'You seem a bit out of it.' To which I would respond more emphatically, 'No, I'm fine.' He'd then switch the conversation topic and ask me, probingly, 'How much sleep are you getting?' I would respond truthfully that it wasn't enough, and then cut off his further attempts to inquire more deeply into the topic.

This conversation repeated itself for months, until finally, one day – after he'd asked me for the hundredth time how much sleep I was getting – I gave him a real answer out of sheer annoyance. This time, I looked straight at him and said, 'I sleep all night. I sleep all day. And when I'm awake, all I can think about is sleep.' In other words, I gave him my first direct answer since I'd started taking Seroquel.

He looked at me, pleased that he finally had a straight answer. He said the Seroquel dosage probably needed to be adjusted and that the sleepiness I was experiencing was quite common on the drug. He added that it would pass when we found the right dose for me.

As far as managing my – as he phrased it – "more problem" symptoms (Dr. Guterson never used the word "psychotic" when discussing my symptoms), we both agreed the new drug combination was pretty effective.

Poof! Just like that, with one conversation and with a few dose adjustments, I wasn't sleeping in my clothes for six hours in the middle of the day anymore.

I'd suffered for so many months because I was too terrified of rejection to tell him I couldn't function on the Seroquel. And yet he'd never judged me about why it took me so long to tell him. He just dealt with the problem at hand and I learned something new about him: that he would believe me.

Dr. Guterson's promise that "we would get through this together" was being proven true, one therapeutic challenge at a time. We were getting through the maze of my complex illnesses together.

When I remember the early years of our journey, I marvel at just how often he made the right clinical judgements even though I was of very little help. I was starting to get at least an inkling that he was a very different MD than I was accustomed to dealing with. I still hadn't come to the understanding that I wasn't living up to my responsibilities in this relationship. That "aha" moment would be birthed in dramatic fashion years into our relationship.

CHAPTER 4

Baby steps

'Dr. Guterson, I don't know if I am capable of healing.'

'You will, in baby steps.'

Every time my soul fell into a crevasse so vast there seemed no escape, I would hear, almost as an echo, his words. 'Baby steps.'

I knew he meant that if I couldn't absorb the enormity of a change he was cajoling me toward, I could take at least a tiny step in its direction. The first and most crucial step I needed to take was that I had to start really talking to him. Sure, I had a therapist I did talk to, but my therapist wasn't male and didn't have an MD after her name.

Dr. Guterson had the potential to be a trustworthy listener. But I hadn't given him much to listen to. If my life was going to evolve into something beyond endless cycles of trauma reactions, psychotic episodes, and suicidal depressions, I needed to learn to talk to him. So what was stopping me? Why did the words that so readily formed in my head never find a voice with him?

*

Late one sweltering summer evening in 1998, when Katie was tucked under her *Little Mermaid* sheets dreaming of Pokémon, I was alone downstairs with a soothing cup of British-style tea. I played a game inside my head. I imagined Dr. Guterson sitting across the living room from me in my antique Cherrywood rocking chair, no notepad, no clinical demeanor, just him sipping tea with me and listening.

In that moment, the words poured out. I told him about the stable of caretakers from my childhood who left indelible and excruciating scars on my body and soul. I told him about the parade of physicians who passed through my life and yet had left the root causes of my traumas untouched. I told him about the steady diet of humiliation forced down my throat. I dipped into my well of shame so that he could see the tears that filled it. I spoke of isolation, desperation, and aloneness.

Most intimately, I spoke about terror – the kind of terror that can drive a person mad if they try to explore its depths. I had so many words to share with him, but no voice to speak them with.

As I broke from my Dr. Guterson trance, a deep pang of loss washed over me. Looking around my living room, I surveyed its contents. The earth-tone couch on which I often curled my feet, the overstuffed chocolate brown chairs Katie liked to bounce on, the smoked glass coffee table that doubled as a dining room table on really bad days, and the rocking chair I had soothed my fussy baby in: they'd all come from Sue. She was all over my house. Her ghost haunted the clothes in my closet and the perfume tucked in my jewelry box. My thoughts about opening up to Dr. Guterson were crowded out by the tangible remnants of Sue.

My eyes gazed downward in despair. The giant red Kool-Aid stain on my rust carpet pulled me away from the dark place I was drifting into. Katie had spilled her cup on the carpet a while back. The spilled drink left a Rorschach-test-like pattern in the middle of the carpet.

I didn't mind the Kool-Aid design. Katie's spirit was a perfect antidote to Sue's shadow. Besides, my little daughter's tender soul was almost impossible for me to find anger with. I remember telling my tearful child as I sopped up the sweet liquid, 'Don't worry, it'll make a pretty pattern when it's dry. Maybe we can figure out what it looks like.' I had scooped her up and blown a raspberry on her cheek, and she'd squealed in delight. That memory brought my soul a rare smile.

That smile vanished when I returned to the present and looked over at the empty rocking chair. Dr. Guterson was not sitting in it, and I wept at the very real possibility that the words in my head might never find his ears.

I went to the kitchen and took my bedtime cocktail of Dr. Guterson's prescribed medications. The walk up the stairs to my bedroom seemed just too daunting to try in the furnace that was my house. So, still in my clothes, I curled up on the couch and drifted into a drug-induced sleep. The faces of my tormentors drifted in and out of my semi-conscious brain. The disjointed voices of my demons taunted me. I sat bolt upright in a panic. My college dorm room attacker was coming. Memories of that brutal night in 1979 flooded my consciousness.

The lanky, dark-haired teenager cussed at me, 'Jezebel. Whore. Satan's spawn.'

He had leapt on top of me before I could even grasp his presence in my dorm room. Yanking my dark brown hair up by its roots, he pinned my head back against the pillow. 'Die, bitch, die,' he shrieked at me. He was pulling my head back so hard that I was struggling to breathe. He lifted up my pink flannel nightgown and injured me.

I didn't scream because I knew, from experience, how to behave when assaulted. I thought to myself, Don't invite more violence. Don't aggravate him. Hang in there till it's over. Endure, that's the key, endure.

He slowly released his death grip on my hair and just sat on my stomach for a few minutes, hissing 'Jezebel' over and over again. Eventually, he lifted himself off me, locked my dorm room door, sat on my roommate's empty bed, and taunted me. 'You are a harlot, a Moabite woman [a biblical reference] *sent to seduce me. I will dismember you, cut open your abdomen, and let your guts pour out onto the floor.'*

Yet, I didn't panic. Rather, I cajoled him with gentle questions about his life. He momentarily smiled and told me a story about his dog. Slowly, I rose from my bed and retreated to the door at the same time that he was grabbing my roommate's extension cord. Suddenly, I felt the cord on the back of my neck but was able to wrench my neck out of its reach. I kicked him, hard, and escaped. Once again, I was the survivor of someone else's psychotic delusion.

I came to and realized I was in my living room. It was 1998, not 1979. But panic had set in. I knew the house wasn't secure. He was coming back. I was sure of it. The alarm bells in my head blared out. I thought about Katie, innocently asleep with her bunny. I sprang into action. I moved the heavy overstuffed chairs and barred the front door. I cut coils of wire and rigged shut every window on the ground level. I only had window fans to make the house bearable, but I couldn't let the monster in. Katie was depending on me. I wedged a dining room chair under the doorknob of the kitchen.

There, I thought, *no one can come in that door.* I grabbed a butcher knife from my knife block and stealthily descended into the basement. I checked every nook and cranny, ready to stab anyone that would leap out and threaten my precious dreamer.

I was determined that Katie would never suffer the hell I lived. I would keep her cocooned in a space of utter safety. If that meant I stayed watchful every night for the duration of her childhood, that's what had to happen. So after my security measures were put in place, I sat on the couch, clutching the butcher knife, listening vigilantly for any sound from outside that portended a threat, and waited for the monster to arrive. One hour drifted into another, and the next sound I heard was the faint beeping of my alarm clock.

It was 6am and he'd never turned up. I had beaten him off, at least this once. Triumphantly, I placed the knife back in its wooden block and walked into Katie's room to wake her for summer camp. I playfully tickled her awake with White Bunny, and she giggled. A new day had begun.

*

By this time, Dr. Guterson and I had been together for a number of years. And yet, he didn't know me, not really. He didn't know what tormented me at night. He didn't know what kept me shut out from the world during the day. Most importantly, he didn't know just how thoroughly I had deliberately kept him from knowing these things. He was magnificent at crisis management. He kept me properly medicated. He made it possible for me to parent. He pushed me when I needed to be pushed. He was the designated keeper of my hope.

However, I didn't trust him enough to tell him about the demons that menaced my nights and shadowed my days. He bore the brunt of the sins of a long line of physicians in my life. I was punishing Dr. Guterson for the crimes committed by those that came before him. I knew what I was doing was wrong on many levels. And I knew that it was time for a "baby step" toward sharing words with him. He was worthy and I needed to tell him what had happened, not only that night but all nights that had come before.

I had an epiphany: if I couldn't get the words to pass my lips, could I get the words to pass through a pen onto paper? So, the next night, while Katie dreamed of Pikachu, I pulled out a yellow legal pad and a blue Bic pen, and I tried to write my first sentences to him about what had happened the night the monster tried to break in.

But it turned out to be harder than I'd initially thought it would be. I'd write some words and, in disgust, rip the page out and tear it up. I tried writing a brief history, a kind of historical timeline. The words would come out cold, sterile, and professorial. I tried writing artistically. It read like a piece of fiction and not the deepest parts of my life experience. I tried writing from a place of emotion. The agony it unleashed was just too crushing. I gave up and felt utterly defeated. I tossed the legal pad and pen back on the bookshelf, sat in the rocking chair, and sobbed. There seemed no escape from the legacy of my past. Even the written word had failed me.

I had an appointment with Dr. Guterson the following afternoon. I had made up my mind; no matter what, I was going to tell him all about the night the demon from my past tried to storm my house.

Unfortunately, the conversation did not match my determination.

He was in a particularly good mood that day. I thought, *Good, maybe this conversation won't be so hard.* As I eased into the conversation with chatter about inconsequential topics, he smiled and said, 'You look like you're doing great.'

I sucked in my breath. 'Actually, I'm having a really hard time,' I said. 'Everything scares me right now and I haven't slept much lately.'

'Are you taking your medications?' he asked.

'Yes,' I responded, teary-eyed. 'But I'm too scared to sleep at night, so I don't.'

Dr. Guterson looked at me, unconcerned. He gave a small shrug. 'From my perspective, you really are doing pretty well. You've had sleeplessness before. It passes. You have a difficult time accepting when things are going well.'

Tears began streaming down my cheeks. I felt obliterated, a non-person. Dr. Guterson looked completely baffled by my reaction. All my instincts in that moment screamed *escape* so I bolted out of his office before the session was even half over. I dove into my stiflingly hot car and slumped over the steering wheel, weeping.

I felt completely invalidated and it reinforced my secret terror that he couldn't be trusted to really care about my trauma. I was devastated. I had tried so hard to tell him about the night the demon came. His response convinced me that he really was indifferent to my anguish, just as I had feared. I took this session as absolute proof that I could not share my really painful trauma experiences with him. I had tried an experiment and the results were negative. Between sniffles, I promised myself I would never try that again.

However, with the passage of time and his steady therapeutic nudging, I did try again.

Over the intervening months, as I calmed down, I had to admit that I had done a horrible job communicating with him. Dr. Guterson had many wonderful qualities, but mind-reading wasn't one of them. True, I had made a Herculean effort to find the right words, but the fact was that the only ones that came out weren't at all descriptive of my problem. He had no way of knowing how hard I was trying, and that what I said and how I said it were the best I could do. I started to wonder if maybe it would be easier to try a different method of communication. I somehow needed to find a way to speak to him that would make it possible for him to really know me. The spoken word was never going to work, so that led me right back to the written word.

I took a step back from the emotion of the problem and put my scientist hat on. It was a bit dusty from being in storage all these years, but if the problem at hand was that I gave Dr. Guterson bad data, I needed to design an experiment that gave him better data. I looked deep into the devastation that was my life to locate the most fundamental piece of information I needed him to know. Then I used supporting evidence to reinforce that critical information. I knew I couldn't share over three decades of trauma in one essay, but I could start with the fundamental problem: my absolute certainty that if he really knew what had been done to me over the years, he would abandon me just like Dr. X and Dr. Q.

So, on a yellow legal pad with one of Katie's gel pens, I started to write. I made the following opening statement:

I absolutely believed that if you knew what had been done to me from childhood to adulthood, you would be indifferent, tell me I'm hopeless, or call me a liar. I believed you would throw me away just like Sue and Dr. Q did. I could not live through being abandoned ... again ... by another physician or therapist. So I stayed silent.

I was putting a stake through the heart of the "Tova Doctrine". That long list of "don't tells" was about to be violated one by one. I wrote to him about my injuries and long-ignored misery. I wrote in detail about my tangled and destructive relationship with Sue. I wrote to him about Dr. Q not being curious about Sue. I wrote about the last and final straw: Dr. X. I wrote it all down, and I cried. As I did, I felt the full force of the abuse and neglect I had endured. I thought about all the time lost with Katie and the loss of my promising science career. I grieved for the person I could have been if these people had just done their damn jobs in the first place. Then I concluded with an apology to him:

My relationship with you is the single most healing, bonding, and enduring relationship I have ever had with anyone. You deserved better from me. You deserved the truth. I'm sorry it has taken so many years to share it.

*

I knew I wanted to read this letter to him. So I took the unusual step of calling him and asking if he could make extra session time for me. I told him I had something crucial to share and I needed time in which to share and discuss with him. He said, 'Sure, no problem,' and he gave me 30 minutes at my appointment the next month. In that time, I must have read and reread my essay two dozen times. I timed it. I practiced it so that I wouldn't get lost in my own words. I also wanted to know that I could get through the entire essay without crumbling. I had to present this to him without being sucked into the traumas I was attempting to share. This essay and this appointment were at the epicenter of my future treatment and our relationship. I was not going to make the same mistake I made all those many months ago when I tried to describe to him the night the demon tried to break in. I had to get this right.

Wednesday afternoon, at my appointed time, I arrived at Dr. Guterson's office. I could walk into his waiting area blindfolded and I'd know every inch of the room. He has this impressionist painting of a 20th century couple walking in the woods. You don't see their faces but you can tell they're enjoying each other's company. The painting is in gentle blue, green, yellow, and pink pastels. I'd stare at it when I was scared, vulnerable, or depressed because the couple looked so serene and the scene was so inviting. On the opposite wall from the painting hang Dr. Guterson's medical license, board certification, and completion of residency. It was good to know he really was an MD. The thought of him actually being an undercover plumber amused me. The walls are completely white. The upholstered seat chairs are comfortable.

His office manager, who sits behind a sliding glass window, greeted me. I was there so often that she knew me just by my voice. I liked Mary. We'd sometimes chat about nothing in particular; the weather, traffic, upcoming weekend plans, holidays, etc. She became a fixture in my life, a constancy when my world was so inconsistent. If I had to call, she would know who I was before I even identified myself. She'd accepted my word when I said something was urgent or, conversely, when I said the topic wasn't urgent but I still needed to speak with her boss. She was professional, respectful, and friendly, and I truly appreciated her for that.

That particular day, I spent a little extra time chatting with Mary. I needed the distraction or else I'd be in a full panic before Dr. Guterson came out of his office. I heard the door to the inner sanctum open and there was Dr. Guterson, looking very comfortable in his pullover shirt and khakis. He greeted me warmly and told me to come in.

'So, what's up?' Dr. Guterson said.

I took a deep breath, unclenched my hands, and shook them before responding. 'I've written something for you and it's really important to me that you hear me.'

He looked intrigued and asked, 'Do you want me to read it?'

I shook my head. 'No, I want to read it to you. It's a bit long, which is why I wanted extra time. Thank you for making time for me, by the way.'

'My pleasure. I really want to hear what you have to say.'

I took another deep breath and pulled out my yellow legal pad. My hands were trembling. I was so grateful I'd practiced reading this so many times. I took one last slow inhalation and looked up at him. He had that look he got when he was completely engaged. It was a mixture of pensiveness and intensity.

I began to read to him. My voice broke a couple of times. An unbidden tear fell on the legal pad. I lost my place once every so often but, for the most part, I got every word out and I didn't crumble. When I closed my legal pad and got the courage to look at his face, I saw compassion and almost tenderness. I started to weep freely.

He responded gently. 'Tova, I had no idea you had been through so much. I am so sorry you have been put through all this.'

I wiped my eyes with the back of my hand. 'You didn't know because I never told you,' I answered him. 'I'm ashamed by that. You deserved better.'

'This is deep, painful stuff,' he responded with great sincerity. 'You have no reason to be ashamed. You shared when you were ready to share. Today you were ready. Last year you weren't.'

I was so relieved. 'Does it help you to know?' I asked.

'Absolutely,' he answered. 'So many things make so much more sense now. This is a huge step for you.'

At that, I started to gather up my things.

'Do you want to talk some more?' he asked. 'We still have some time.'

I felt completely spent. Almost with a sigh, I responded, 'Not right now. I need to sit with this for a while. I feel completely wrung out.'

'Will you write more for me?' he asked.

I instantly perked up. 'Really, you want me to? Yes! This works. I can talk to you like this.' I beamed at him, and he beamed right back at me.

Normally, I would walk out of his office looking down at my feet. I'd avoid the gaze of people casually passing by me in the parking lot. I'd keep my head down, my dark hair covering my face. On that day, I raised my head, tucking my hair behind my ears. It was a cloudy fall afternoon and the smell of rain was in the air, but all I felt was sunshine. A stranger smiled at me; gazing at his smile, I smiled back. Another baby step.

CHAPTER 5

DR. GUTERSON!

I got the job!

We'd been together for over a decade. Most of that time, I was so fragile that all Dr. Guterson and I could manage was to build up my inner resources and find the right medications to complement my emerging stability.

One day, out of the blue on a routine appointment, he declared, 'Tova, you need to have intellectual stimulation. You should think about going back to school and picking up another degree. It doesn't matter what you study, you just need to have your mind engaged.'

I knew he was spot on. I had done no heavy intellectual lifting since that day in 1994 when my lab director placed me on disability leave. It was now 2004. The intervening ten years had resulted in brain rot. Aside from assisting Katie with her homework, I don't recall participating in a single activity that used my intellect.

The idea of going back to school intrigued and terrified me. Once upon a time I had been a gifted student and scientist. Now those memories and experiences belonged to a very different human being.

But if Dr. Guterson was confident I could take this challenge on, I was going to prove him right.

The first hurdle, and it was a huge one, was finding the resources to return to school. The crushing reality was that I was living on disability insurance. In those intervening years, as I healed and stabilized, Katie had grown from a timid first-grader clutching her bunny at our reunion, to a confident and gifted teenager I'd occasionally spar with. She was in high school and college was around the corner for her. Could I really justify taking on student loans for myself, when we were soon going to need loans for her?

As hard as I might have found it, the answer was yes. I told myself that Katie's financial aid would work itself out. We had four years to plan and she was a talented student. My need was more urgent. I was rotting.

Nancy, my therapist during this time, suggested that I contact our state's disabilities office and find out what resources were available for education. A polite woman answered the phone and made an intake appointment for me. She told me that the counselor would come to me. The appointment was in three weeks and I chose a coffee shop near my home as the meeting place.

Three weeks gave me a lot of time to cogitate on the impact that returning to college would have on my life. For three weeks, I did my *Hamlet* interpretation for both Dr. Guterson and Nancy. 'To go back or not to go back, that is the question.' The two of them were sympathetic to the fact that I was about to make an enormous life change – and I wasn't gifted at making life changes. However, I had to admit, I was being just a bit melodramatic about the decision. They humored me. I fretted. The three weeks passed.

I sat in the coffee shop anxiously awaiting the arrival of – who exactly? I doubted he'd be wearing a name tag. *What does a vocational counselor even look like?* I sipped tea and wondered. Images of an old, grizzled man in bell-bottom jeans and a tie-dyed shirt popped into my head.

From the corner of my eye, I caught a glimpse of a dark-haired young man in jeans and a white pullover shirt walking through the coffee shop door. He was carrying a large leather satchel across his shoulder. He seemed to be casing the place. *Hmm*, I thought. *He's either looking for someone or planning to rob the shop.* My twisted humor got the best of me. What if he was an armed robber? I'd never get my appointment in and there would be more weeks of *Hamlet*. Well, if he was a criminal I was going to find out.

I approached him. 'Tova?' he said.

'Yep, and I guess you aren't an armed robber.'

He looked totally confused. I apologized and explained myself. He chuckled. 'That's a new one on me,' he said.

We sat down in a booth and got right to business. He asked a lot of questions about my disability and treatment. My answers were honest and forthright. He asked me about my finances. I told him I was on Social Security disability. He asked me what my educational goals were. I told him I wanted to go back to college and earn another degree. Then he asked a question I hadn't prepared an answer to. Staring down at his voluminous checklist, he asked me, in a perfunctory tone, 'Are you planning to return to work with this new degree?'

I had an "aha" moment and responded instinctively, 'Yes. I do plan to go back to work.' I was taken aback by my answer. I had never considered the possibility that working would ever again be in my future.

While I was on pause, he moved to the next question on the list. 'What kind of work do you see yourself doing?'

With pride, I answered, 'Research. I'm a scientist, but I've been out of the field so long I'm obsolete.'

He looked up from his paperwork and stated from rote, 'The vocational office has some requirements before we make a final decision. We need you to fill out a release for your psychiatric and medical records. We'll also need you to fill out the detailed application I have for you. And we'll need you to take an IQ test.'

I was puzzled by his last item. 'An IQ test?'

'Yes,' he answered flatly. 'We need to verify that college is appropriate for you.'

I looked at him incredulously and stammered, 'I did my graduate school work in toxicology and biochemistry and my undergraduate work in chemistry.'

He shrugged, and assumed a very bureaucratic tone. 'We insist on an IQ test. We need to know that you can do the work.'

My pride a little hurt, I decided to get cheeky with this guy. 'Which measuring instrument do you use?'

He looked at me oddly. 'Huh?'

'Do you use the Stanford-Binet instrument or another one? There are others.'

Peevishly, he responded, 'I don't know. Just show up for the exam.'

He had half a dozen forms for me to sign and he gave me my application packet. It was due in ten days. I thanked him for his time and told him how appreciative I was that he wasn't a robber. He couldn't help himself and chuckled again. *At least he's leaving on a positive note,* I thought to myself.

I couldn't wait to share with Dr. Guterson the details of my encounter with a real-life bureaucrat. At our appointment later that week, he asked how it'd gone with the vocational counselor.

I gave him a disgusted look and said, 'He thinks I might be too stupid to go to college. I have to take an IQ test. I hate that guy.'

Dr. Guterson rolled his eyes. Almost conspiratorially he said, 'Knock his socks off.'

'Oh, I will,' I said. I was ready for battle.

*

In a rare display of ego, I was genuinely insulted that this guy had insisted I take an IQ test. After all, one of the few positive hold-overs from childhood was that I knew I was really smart. However, since I needed this agency's help to achieve a greater goal, I would just swallow my pride and jump through their hoops.

I got all the paperwork in on time. Mary got all my psychiatric records to them, and I showed up for my IQ test. They put me through the standard Stanford-Binet battery: general knowledge questions, block design, number retention, verbal skills, etc. And I breezed through it, like I knew I would.

The examiner looked at me quizzically. 'That was fast.'

'It wasn't hard,' I replied snottily.

The only thing left to do was wait for the final judgement, which came a few weeks later.

My vocational counselor called me and, in an uncharacteristically conciliatory tone, said, 'Tova, we got your IQ test results back. Why didn't you tell me?'

This was the moment I was waiting for. Victory was in the air. 'Because you would never have believed me,' I said.

'I've never had a client like you. What exactly would you like to study and what degree are you planning to pursue?'

I could barely hold back my pride at having battled and won. I responded, in a softer tone than before, 'In a perfect world, I'd like to earn my doctorate in biochemistry. In an imperfect world, I'd settle for another bachelor's degree, maybe in psychology.'

The counselor paused for a minute. 'Vocational services have never funded a doctorate before ... but you're a special case, so I can try.'

I recognized an ally when I heard one. 'I'd be grateful for anything you can offer. A doctorate is my dream,' I said humbly.

'Tova, there is no harm in asking,' he reassured me.

The answer came a month later: "no" to the doctorate, "yes" to the bachelor's. I was okay with the decision. Vocational services sweetened the deal by offering me complete funding for tuition, supplies, and books. I wouldn't need a loan unless I wanted one for living expenses.

I had tangled with a bureaucracy and won. I couldn't wait to share my victory with Dr. Guterson.

This was, after all, his idea.

*

Dr. Guterson had been on vacation, so I hadn't seen him in the intervening month or so since that initial interview with the vocational counselor. I had a lot to catch him up on.

I shared my success with him at my next appointment. 'Vocational services are completely funding my second bachelor's degree. I tried for a doctorate, but they don't fund doctorates.'

Dr. Guterson looked genuinely delighted. 'Tova, that's fantastic! What became of the IQ test hassle?'

Smug with satisfaction, I answered, 'I knocked their socks off.'

Dr. Guterson chuckled. 'I never had a doubt.'

We both sat silently and absorbed the enormity of this breakthrough in my treatment. I could have sat in his office and basked in the glow of his excitement for the length of another session. Unfortunately, our 15 minutes were up, and I had to get on with all the preparations I needed to make.

*

I enrolled at the large public university in our city. Student life was just as harrowing as I remembered it. There was the usual stuff such as finding parking, locating buildings, meeting professors, etc. Then there was the unusual stuff. I was too large to fit in many lecture hall seats, I was old enough to be the mom of almost every student in class, and I was computer-illiterate. I'd had no reason to go near a computer in all the years I was unemployed, which meant I was out of my league with 2004 technology.

To make matters worse, my isolation came along with me for company. I sat alone in lecture halls, ate alone, studied alone, and walked to class alone. However, I was still a gifted student and the professors took notice. I was never late, always attended class, completed every assignment on time, did extra credit, asked thought-provoking questions, and excelled. My academic advisor managed to condense the four-year BS psychology program into two-and-a-half years for me. This was largely because I had so many credits on my various transcripts from my other degrees, the only subject courses I needed were psychology courses and one public speaking course, which I dreaded.

Those were fairly stable years for me. I went to class every day, saw my therapist twice a week, saw Dr. Guterson twice a month, and watched Katie blossom into a confident and brilliant high school student in her own right. I had no hospitalizations for this entire period of time. Dr. Guterson's recommendation that I return to school was perfectly timed to suit my newly emerged stability. Our efforts were paying off.

After class one afternoon, one of my professors, Dr. Richards, asked me to stop by her office. I liked Dr. Richards a lot. She was an older woman, close to my age with graying hair, and she was a little overweight. As we sat in her office drinking diet sodas together, we discussed challenges that moms with nearly adult children face.

She told me she was a bit discouraged by the quality of student now entering college. She lamented that she didn't see students who were hungry to learn and willing to work anymore. She looked up from her soda can and said, 'Students like you, Tova.'

Her words truly touched me. Then, as I continued to sit and sip with her, she asked me, 'Would you be interested in a part-time research assistantship? It doesn't pay much, only $12.00 an hour, but the experience will be priceless to you as you change research specialties.'

I tried to contain my excitement and feigned an academic's demeanor, asking about the study thesis.

'A friend of mine over at the medical school has an ongoing study of older patients with diabetes. It's a medication compliance study. It has both a behavioral component and a biomedical component. If you're interested, I'll give her your name and contact information. I know that she'll hire you based on my recommendation.'

I felt as if I had been struck by lightning. I could barely contain my enthusiasm. 'Please. I would be so grateful. Do you need my resume?'

'Sure, I can pass that along to her. Can you fax it?'

'Consider it done,' I said. *But first*, I thought to myself, *I need to find it.* After so many years of decay, I knew my resume was in serious need of an overhaul.

We continued to sip diet soda and the topic moved to our foreign travels. I silently pinched myself as we spoke. Here I was, enjoying the company of an intelligent, accomplished woman near my age and never once did I hear – or have to say – anything about being severely mentally ill. I'd have to check with Dr. Guterson, of course, but this had all the markings of normalcy.

"Normal" had been a very long time ago for me. I began to spiral into my own thoughts as I sat there. It wasn't that I saw Dr. Richards as my friend. Rather, she was the first non-clinical, non-mentally ill, new acquaintance I had made since 1994. She didn't know anything about my tortured history and I wanted to keep it that way. Our chat served to remind me that I could be thought of as intelligent and interesting even with a mental illness. My secret terror was that I wouldn't be able to hold up to this image.

*

I paced the floor in Dr. Guterson's waiting room. A job. I was contemplating getting a *job* in research. My mood jumped from euphoria to abject terror and back to euphoria.

Dr. Guterson caught me mid-pace. He gave me a look as if he was expecting to deal with an emerging crisis. In his firm clinical voice, he called my name and ushered me into his office. I didn't even give him a chance to speak. Before sitting down, I dove right in to the subject at hand. Pacing and talking, I blurted out, 'I was offered a chance at a job in research.'

Dr. Guterson, recognizing the clinical significance of my declaration, responded calmly, 'Fill me in.'

Pacing and babbling, I told him that my professor, Dr. Richards, had invited me to apply for a research assistantship at the medical school. 'I've got all these conflicting thoughts and feelings rushing through my head. I'm terrified I'm going to ruin this opportunity. I'm also ecstatic that I may, after all these years, have a job again in science. What if I'm not ready to try this? What if I'm never ready?'

Dr. Guterson's tone was measured. 'Tell me about the position.' His quiet demeanor settled me and I finally sat down.

'It's part-time, $12 an hour, studying medication noncompliance. I'll be working directly with study participants and collecting neurocognitive data among other data points.'

He probed gently. 'What worries you the most about taking this job?'

I didn't hesitate in responding. 'Failure.'

He paused and put his pen down on his notes. 'Tova, if you weren't terrified of failure after everything you have been through, I would be far more concerned. I believe that you're ready for this step. Easing you back into full-time employment isn't going to be an event; it's a process. We're at the beginning of that process. Do you want to be employed?'

Again, I didn't need to think for a second. 'Yes. without a doubt. I just don't know if I'm ready. I don't know what to do. I'm paralyzed.'

'Do you want my opinion?'

'Uh-huh.'

'Go for it, Tova,' he said emphatically, grinning at me. 'I'll be right here if you need me.'

I left his office a more complete person than I had entered it. An aspect of myself that I had once thought dead had been resurrected. I was going to be employed in my field of study once again. Somebody wanted me as a professional! No medication could substitute for the sense of wellbeing I felt at the prospect of employment.

*

The study coordinator formally offered me the research assistantship. It was rough going at first. I second-guessed every decision I made and didn't trust my instincts. With every small error I felt certain that my budding career would end.

I did well with the patients but not as well with my coworkers. I couldn't be social. I was still struggling with my competence. Every time I'd declare to Dr. Guterson, 'I can't do this,' he'd redirect me and point out that I actually was doing it. He would tell me to just keep doing what I was doing. In other words, more baby steps.

I worked at this study for two years until the project was completed. My zeal for employment had soared by this point. After a carefully orchestrated job search, I landed my next part-time medical research position. This time I would be working in the private sector. Many of the interpersonal challenges I faced at my reentry job had begun to work themselves out by the time I entered my second job. I was more confident, had acquired better computer skills, and was ready for the competitive world of private sector research. As I continued to push my professional limits, my sense of competence evolved.

Then, finally, I was given the opportunity to apply for a full-time professional research position at a nonprofit biomedical foundation. I met the challenge and got the position.

My reentry into the world of employment began in 2004. By 2010, I was full-time employed and off Social Security disability. Every step along the way, Dr. Guterson encouraged me. Every stumble during that transition, he helped pick me up and dust me off. I told him once, that work should be labeled as medicine. Its healing power is tremendous. Work provided me with structure, purpose, human contact, worth, and financial independence – in other words, wellbeing.

After experiencing the benefits of gainful employment after a decade of disability, I told him I would never ever go back to disability again. That's not to say I ceased to be ill or ceased to be relapse-prone. In fact, I've had several severe relapses while employed. But despite these setbacks, I have held tight to my professional life. It is a fact that I need to work just as much as I need to take Dr. Guterson's cocktail of medications.

As I made this declaration, Dr. Guterson beamed at me. He looked genuinely proud of me, and wow, did that feel amazing.

CHAPTER 6

Tova,

WE HAVE A PROBLEM

'Tova, if you were a patient I was meeting for the first time, there is no way I would consider releasing you. I think I need to take a step back and rethink what's going on with you.'

Dr. Guterson's words froze me mid-plea. I stood before him, weighing 108 pounds, refusing to swallow anything, and manic. But I truly didn't see any problem. I had been trying to convince him of this fact since my – as I saw it – coerced admission into hospital. I badgered him constantly to release me. Hospitals were for people who were struggling to keep themselves safe or who were psychotic. I was perfect in every way. In fact, I was a star in the firmament–magical, omnipotent, and omniscient. Why would Dr. Guterson not want me to leave the hospital and fulfill my mission as G-d's emissary on Earth? Why would he be so stern in the face of so much perfection?

I was truly baffled. My only conclusion was that he wasn't as brilliant as I had thought he was. I was in no mood to humor him, however. G-d had sent me to eradicate malignant alternate dimensional forces that had invaded the Earth, and every minute I was kept locked up was one less minute spent stopping an earthquake in Nepal or a tornado in Kansas. He was keeping me from saving lives, and that really ticked me off. People could die while I was stuck in the hospital!

This episode had its roots three years earlier, in 2009. Understanding the crisis would take me, Dr. Guterson, and my new psychologist Lynn a whole additional year to have a collective "aha" moment. In the meantime, severe mania and psychosis had returned.

I had been mania-free for over a decade. 'Why now? What had changed?' Dr. Guterson questioned me. My medications hadn't changed. Yes, I had a new therapist, Lynn, but changing therapists doesn't make one manic after so many years of being symptom-free. Katie was in college and doing absolutely wonderfully. I had been employed full-time for going on two years, and I had adjusted well. There was only one event in my life that could have been the cause of this massive disruption In 2009, I had had gastric bypass surgery. How gastric bypass surgery (GBS) might be connected to the return of bipolar symptoms, we had yet to discover.

*

In the spring of 2008, I weighed 310 pounds. Food had become my source of comfort as I struggled with isolation, loneliness, and self-revulsion. However, I had grown too large to sit in an airplane seat or go to a theater. I even had to wedge myself behind the steering wheel of my car in order to drive. Total strangers would scream 'Jenny Craig!' out their car windows at me as I hobbled down the street. If I were in a crowd, people would avert thier gaze as if my weight were somehow contagious. The more shame that was heaped on me, the more I lived in denial about the problem.

I became reclusive. I only left the house to see Dr. Guterson and work at the local university. I had no social life. I had a work life, a treatment life, and animals. Katie's cat Rosebud and dog Frodo were sort of bequeathed to me when she left for college. I had never been comfortable around animals. They always seemed so vulnerable to me. However, they would prove to be my sole source of comfort at 3am during dark times.

Even as I excelled academically, I built walls around me socially. Growing up, Katie had always been remarkably accepting of my size.

I had always been morbidly obese to her. When she was little and other children would taunt her about my weight, she'd yell at them.

'My mom isn't fat, she's fluffy!'

The fact that my little daughter had to defend me to bullies mortified me and further thrust me into shamed denial. Dr. Guterson tried on multiple occasions to gently nudge a discussion about my weight, but I always shut him down. My psychologist was more aggressive. All she did was drive me deeper into self-revulsion. My family physician told me I wasn't going to live to see my daughter graduate from college. I guess he thought that scaring me into losing weight was a smart strategy. All he managed to do was make me wonder if that really was all that terrible an outcome. I remember thinking of "death by Twinkie", and the twisted thought made me giggle.

Death in the abstract, when every day is an endurance test, does have its appeal. Death as an imminent likelihood is a bit more complex. One night I was lying on my side, trying to sleep, when I felt a crushing pain in my chest. I couldn't catch my breath and I was sweating profusely. My first thought was, *I guess the PCP had a point.*

As I lay in bed, struggling to breathe, I gave thought to just letting nature take its course. I was completely worn out from fighting so long and so hard with life. Katie was no longer a child. I had done my job.

At that point, I had more or less settled on death by Twinkie. But when it came right down to actually embracing that fate, I bailed on bailing. The responsible thing would have been to call 911. However, I was enormous. I wasn't going to go through that humiliation. Instead, I drove myself to the hospital.

The term "invasive" doesn't even begin to describe all the poking, prodding, injecting, and monitoring that went on in our community hospital's ER. When all the data was collected and analyzed, the attending cardiologist came in and told me the news. I had a rather large thoracic aortic aneurysm and a leaking aortic valve.

He couldn't leave it at that. He had to add that it was caused by "years of chronic, untreated, severe hypertension". He went on to say that they were consulting a cardiovascular surgeon and my case was "complicated". My interpretation: I was so fat they didn't know what to do with me. I was admitted to the cardiac floor to stabilize and wait for the surgeon. The nurse came in and asked me if there was anyone I'd like her to call. As I thought about it, the honest answer was "no". There was no one to call. Katie was happily adjusting to college and I wasn't going to bother her with this. I had no friends. I had no family. Such was the reality of my life.

You'd think that I had experienced enough humiliation for one day. But no, I just hadn't met the surgeon yet. As he strode into my room, without him saying a word, I knew he was the surgeon. He was the stereotype of every television doctor I had ever seen. He had graying hair at the temples, a crisp white lab coat, stethoscope shoved in his coat pocket, and green scrubs.

He talked not even at me; he talked past me. I think he was actually trying to communicate with the nondescript piece of abstract art hanging behind my bed. I was already in as vulnerable a position as I could be. I was this amorphous blob lying on this bed in only a hospital gown. There were machines that went ping all around me, creating endless amounts of data that I really didn't want to know about. There was no supportive person on my side to stare this guy down. I lay there essentially naked and helpless, listening to him talk past me with contempt.

In a perfunctory tone, the surgeon said, 'Normally we'd go in and surgically repair the valve and the aneurysm. However, you're too great a surgical risk and you have a better chance of dying during surgery than as a result of the aneurysm.'

His callousness made me shiver. 'What happens now?' I asked meekly.

Engrossed in his fingernails, he muttered, 'Manage you medically. Monitor you closely. And you either lose weight or you die of a ruptured aneurysm. You should consider gastric bypass surgery.'

I was perplexed. 'I thought I was too great a surgical risk?'

He rolled his eyes as if I had asked a moronic question. 'Yes, to have your chest cracked open, your heart stopped, and the repairs done.'

Ouch, I thought. *That was uncalled for.* But I pressed on with my questions. 'Do you have a recommendation for a gastric bypass surgeon?'

Even as I was forming my words, he turned his back to me and headed for the door. I listened to the back of his head respond, 'Do research. Ask your PCP. Any other questions?'

Of course, I had more questions. But he was done answering. He walked out, leaving me in shamed silence. All I wanted to do was escape from that hospital and hide out at home where Katie's cat and dog, my only friends, were. I thought about calling Dr. Guterson, to fill him in, but I wondered why he would care about this. No call was made.

I stayed in the hospital another few days and they released me with discharge instructions and a referral to the city's most respected cardiovascular surgery clinic. I had an appointment for the next day. I left the hospital with a brand-new set of diagnoses and an unavoidable problem on my hands. If I really didn't want to die, my weight issue would have to be resolved. I started to cry. Before my odyssey into mental health-care, I'd maintained a stable, healthy weight. Now, 12 years later, I was too fat to have an aneurysm repaired. Were my only options to be fat, sane, and dead or skinny, alive, and crazy?

I met with my new cardiovascular surgeon the next day. I sat waiting in the clinic for hours. I'd no sooner fill out one piece of paper than five more magically appeared. There had to be 50 people in that waiting room and I doubted there were 50 physicians waiting to see them.

People were scattered all over the expansive room. Some were quietly talking to companions or watching a mindless talk show on the television, while others were just staring into space. I opted for staring into space. The physician's assistant took a detailed history, including a mental health history. I was finally taken back to a very standard examination room where I sat on the paper-covered exam table for more poking and prodding. I was sure I'd hate the surgeon, but I was actually pleasantly surprised. He was a very dignified and respectful slight-of-build Japanese man. Unlike the surgeon at the hospital, he had no trace of condescension in his voice. He reviewed my history and began our conversation with a very odd question.

'Are you mentally unbalanced?'

His question brought out the twisted humor in me. 'Not today, why?'

He continued. 'Gastric bypass surgery is an excellent idea for you, but you will have to discuss it with your psychiatrist. I really can't operate on you unless you lose a tremendous amount of weight. At that point, we'll reevaluate your surgical risk. In the meantime, every six months we have an appointment.'

I asked perhaps an obvious question, but I needed to know. 'How will I know if there's a problem with the aneurysm?'

Dr. K surprised me. 'An excellent question,' he said. 'You'll experience chest pain and shortness of breath like you had before. Come to this hospital by calling 911. Don't drive yourself to the hospital like you did during this last emergency. That was dangerous. Once you get here, the ER will page me.'

I was strangely reassured that if there were to be a crisis, he'd be the one to manage it. I was truly grateful that he treated me like a human being. 'Thank you,' I said. 'You've been kind and very informative.'

He gave me what approached a smile and reiterated his key points: I needed to talk to Dr. Guterson and find a gastric bypass surgeon. If I ran into trouble with the aneurysm, he'd be there to manage it.

Just as he was about to leave, he turned to me and said, 'One more thing: there are three gastric bypass surgery centers we refer patients to. The information will be in your discharge summary.' He wished me well on my hunt for the right surgeon and exited the room.

*

My appointment with Dr. Guterson was fast approaching. I hadn't settled on what I was going to tell him about my adventures with the aneurysm. Everything had happened in between appointments with him. I had 15 minutes to get him up to speed and get his permission for surgery.

I've learned over the years that I can cram a lot of essential information into a short appointment. It's a skill. It also helps to have a strong therapeutic bond with your psychiatrist, because comfort in disclosure speeds up communication. Dr. Guterson knows me well enough that we just get right to business and tackle the issue at hand.

I arrived on time for my appointment with him. In fact, I'm almost always on time. I don't mind if Dr. Guterson is running late. He can't control emergencies, and to be fair, I've caused him to be late on a number of occasions. This was one of those days when he was delayed.

Mary was busy helping someone over the phone, so I took a seat in the waiting room. I gazed at the painting of the couple strolling through the woods. For the first time, I found myself reflecting on the woman's weight. *She's really thin. I wish I could remember what that felt like.* I looked at the end table piled up with assorted magazines. I had never read any of the magazines in Dr. Guterson's waiting room. Actually, their titles were pretty boring.

Wow, I thought to myself, *I really am avoiding the subject at hand if I'm pondering issues of* Home and Garden.

I heard Mary call my name, so I went up to the glass and greeted her. We exchanged pleasantries and she asked me an insurance question. As I was answering, Dr. Guterson came out of his office without my hearing him. He was right behind me and as I turned around, I almost ran into him. He chuckled a bit and said jovially, 'Come on in, Tova.'

It helped when he was in a particularly good mood. I've become an expert over the years in interpreting his vocal tones, facial expressions, body language, and gestures. I'm sure studying your psychiatrist's moods is in the patient handbook for getting the most out of your clinical care.

'So, what's been happening?' he queried.

In an attempt to inject some levity into the upcoming exchange, I responded, 'I've been in the hospital and you weren't the one who put me in there.'

He had a mixture of surprise and concern on his face.

His look told me it was time to be serious, so I gave him a brief synopsis of my adventures with the aneurysm. 'I was admitted to the hospital with heart-related symptoms. I was diagnosed with an ascending thoracic aortic aneurysm and a leaking aortic valve.'

He looked at me pensively. 'How do they plan to treat it?'

I summarized Dr. K's evaluation. 'They can't surgically repair it. I weigh too much to tolerate the surgery. Instead they're following it closely, drastically reducing my blood pressure, and they want me to have gastric bypass surgery to facilitate weight loss. After which, they'll reevaluate my surgical risk.'

'What do you think about all this?'

I felt oddly disconnected from the crisis and my tone reflected that. 'The surgeon didn't leave me with much choice. I'll look for a GBS surgeon who will take my case. Oh, and my cardiovascular surgeon wanted to know if I'm "mentally unbalanced". He was looking at my mental health history.'

The statement was meant to bring some humor to the conversation, but Dr. Guterson was not in the least bit amused by the comment. 'If the surgeon wanted an answer to that question, he should have consulted me.'

I felt strangely protected by his slight indignation. 'He also said I needed your consent to have the surgery.'

He thought for a minute and, with gravity, gave his clinical judgement. 'Your mood has been stable for quite a while. Since your surgeon sees this as medically necessary, I have no reason to object from a psychiatric perspective … at this time.'

I tried to reassure him of my competence to take on this challenge. 'I'm going to interview surgical sites. If I don't like one, I'll move on. I'm going to be picky.'

He was surprisingly relieved that I had a rational plan for evaluating surgical centers and told me he was supportive of my strategy.

A 15-minute appointment turned into almost a 30-minute appointment. I had added to his backlog, and I felt vaguely guilty. I knew other patients were waiting. On reflection, however, I think I did a great job communicating the basics of the problem. I knew that selecting a surgeon was going to take time. Having Dr. Guterson's tentative approval would make the process go a lot smoother.

*

I interviewed all three sites that had been recommended to me. I felt like Goldilocks. One site was cold and impersonal. I sat in an auditorium with 30 other people and listened as the nurse in charge of patient recruitment gave a generic presentation on the surgery. *I'm not vanilla and my situation is not average,* I thought.

At the second site a single surgeon met with me privately. When I gave him my medical and psychiatric history, he said, 'No problem, I'll do a quick work up and I can do the surgery in two weeks.' I thought that either this guy didn't get the complicated nature of my medical problems or he was just interested in the income. Neither was a comforting answer.

I was starting to get discouraged, but I had one more site to evaluate. The third surgery center was very organized and patient-friendly. I met with the intake nurse, the dietician, the physician's assistant, and then the surgeon. He had read all my records, talked to his team, consulted with his partner, and made the decision that he'd take my case. He required that I agree to extensive pre-op testing, obtain an approval letter from my psychiatrist, and have an interview with their psychologist. He told me he knew time was urgent for me, but he wasn't performing surgery until I could show a steady weight loss of 20 pounds. He was evaluating my willingness to follow through with the post-surgery regimen. He also reassured me that because of my unique circumstances, there would be no problem getting insurance company approval. He concluded by admonishing me that the surgery was the easy part. What followed, he stressed, was when the road got tough. As it turned out, more prophetic words were never spoken.

*

I had the surgery in December of 2009. There were no surgical complications and I was obsessively adherent to the post-surgical diet. The weight literally melted off of me. As the weight fell off and the number on the scale started to drop, I found a new obsession. I started to play this game with my food: how little could I eat and how much weight could I shed? I had the surgery in December, and by my one-year anniversary, I was back to my pre-mental healthcare weight.

But suddenly that wasn't good enough. I wanted to be so tiny that I could fit into a size zero. Only months later, I was a size zero.

During this time, I made radical life changes with very little planning. I withdrew from treatment with my long-time psychologist, Nancy. We had been struggling for several years to refocus my treatment after Katie had grown up. I picked this post-GBS moment to end the conflict.

Of course, Dr. Guterson had a different opinion about me terminating therapy and referred me to a new therapist, Lynn. There was a lag time of about six months between when I left Nancy and decided to see Lynn. I was also only seeing Dr. Guterson once every two months at this time.

When you weigh 300 pounds, it takes even the most careful observer a long time to notice that you've crossed the line from losing weight appropriately into anorexia. I was on a constant high from being so thin. I could go to the symphony again. I could board a plane. I could walk for hours and my back and knees didn't hurt. I was full of energy, confidence, and pride. No one would ever yell "Jenny Craig" at me again or call me Shamu. Almost magically, people made eye contact with me again, and for the first time in my life, men flirted with me. I was so high, so energized, I'd flirt right back. I had been transformed. Every trace of self-hatred was gone. No one, I pledged to myself, was ever going to harm, humiliate, or abuse me again. I was the personification of personal empowerment.

As far as the aneurysm was concerned, I was off all three of my blood pressure medications, the aneurysm had not expanded, and the leaking aortic valve that was once so much of a concern suddenly wasn't a concern anymore. My surgeon told me that he'd take routine measurements to be sure the aneurysm wasn't expanding and he'd carefully follow how the valve was functioning. In other words, the plan was for no imminent surgery, just follow-up. He was almost as delighted saying the words as I was in hearing his words. The GBS had done its job.

*

I strolled into Dr. Guterson's office for an appointment one hot July day in 2012. I was sporting white short shorts, a hot pink tank top, and sandals. It wasn't my normal attire, which was somewhat frumpy but modest; this was way out of the norm for me.

I couldn't contain myself in that office. I was pure energy. I had plans, millions of ideas that had hatched inside my head. I began to rattle all my brilliant and creative ideas off to him. I described in great scientific detail how I could cure Ebola with the contents of my spice rack if only I could control alter-dimensional sabotage.

From my time with him, I've learned that Dr. Guterson has levels of clinical intensity. It ranges from casually engaged to "red alert". At this appointment, he was on "red alert". Had I not ignored his intense gaze, monotone cadence, and drop in vocal tone, I could have predicted what was going to come next from him. But I was blissfully and completely unaware that I had crossed into mania.

Thankfully, the transition was not lost on Dr. Guterson. He looked at me with therapeutic concentration and said, 'Tova, we have a problem.'

He admitted me to the hospital that afternoon, indifferent to my manic, ranting objections. This was my first psychiatric admission in almost eight years, and it was going to be a brutal one.

Trigger Warning: This chapter contains references to eating disorders.

CHAPTER 7

Lynn and Dr. Guterson
TEAM TOVA

From my perch in the seclusion room, I screamed, 'No! Stay away! Don't touch me! You are all part of their plot! Don't you see that they've controlled your minds! I'm your only protection against the forces of death and destruction! Please let me do my assigned task from G-d!'

I had climbed up on the radiator ledge in the room, refusing to come down. Everyone who came in to coax me off the ledge had been co-opted by the EVIL ONES. I could tell by the distinct glow of their skin. They were almost zombies, swarming on me and trying to force me to give up my sacred mission. I was invoking the forces of LIGHT to dispel the EVIL that had possessed all of them and they were not in the slightest bit grateful!

The next thing I knew I was being grabbed on both sides and literally forced off my safe stoop. I was now on the same level as the EVIL ONES. THEY had access to me. I pleaded and squirmed. I begged and fought. I crumbled into hysterical, terrified sobs. No one said a word to me. I was surrounded. I was forced onto a bed, injected with something, and restrained. My wrists were bound. My ankles were bound. Whatever they had injected me with made me instantly woozy. I stopped struggling against the restraints. I was reduced to a whimpering puppy. The staff member assigned to stay with me had music playing. I began drifting off into a drug-induced stupor with some Top 40 song as my lullaby. I vaguely remember saying 'Thank you' to the staff person before oblivion set in. I'm sure he had no idea that I was talking about his music.

I awoke to Dr. Guterson gazing down on me. He seemed almost relieved. 'You look a lot better.' He grabbed the aide's vacated chair. 'Do you remember anything?'

Cutting through the fog in my brain, I answered, 'Being restrained and music.' I felt so groggy that it was hard to talk to him. Dr. Guterson reassured me that the staff removed the restraints as soon as I had fallen asleep.

I looked up blankly at him. 'How long have I been asleep?'

'As long as you needed to be.'

A glimmer of my twisted humor crept in. 'That's a non-answer,' I said drowsily.

Dr. Guterson gently deflected my question. 'We can talk details later. For now, let's just take this in baby steps.'

I was so lethargic, I began to drift off. But just before I slipped into sleep, I reminded him, 'I like baby steps.'

I fell asleep after that, feeling safe because of his presence. I was drooling. My eyelids were heavy. My limbs rebelled at moving. I dozed some more.

*

One baby step led to another. Lynn came in for an in-hospital session a few days later. Her petite frame and adherence to Chassidic Judaism's respect for modesty belied a tenacity and compassion that revolutionized my therapy. We had instantly bonded at our first appointment. There was something about her aura. She had a no-nonsense therapeutic approach tempered with a deep, sensitive compassion. I felt cared about and safe in her presence.

With Lynn in charge of my therapy, it was finally time to excavate my long-buried secrets. In just a few months Lynn knew more about my trauma history than Dr. Guterson had learned in our 14 years together. In fact, Lynn even knew about the pesky toddler in my head, a well-hidden secret.

There was also a huge bonus to having Lynn as my psychologist. She and Dr. Guterson worked closely together when they shared patients. She wouldn't be shy about telling him what she felt he needed to know. I could even imagine a scenario where she'd give him treatment advice about me. Tiny Lynn staring down a towering Dr. Guterson – that, I would pay to see. I'd never had a therapist, not even Carrie, who had such a seamless working relationship with him. I didn't realize it at the time, but the introduction of Lynn to my psychiatric relationship would accelerate my healing. She was the catalyst my treatment needed. Together they were now Team Tova.

I was awake when Lynn arrived. She was wearing her customary long black skirt and long-sleeved, high-necked aqua blouse. She greeted me with a 'Hi, dolly' and a smile that warmed my battered soul. I didn't have anything profound to say, but her presence was like aloe vera on a blistering burn. I was so grateful she'd taken the time to have a session with me, even while I was in the hospital. Inpatient units are not always the most comfortable settings for clinicians in private practice, but Lynn took the unit in her stride.

I still had a hangover from the heavy sedation. But for me, at that moment, her presence was enough. I needed no words. She had some words to share with me, though. She wanted to talk about my not eating. It wasn't a deep psychological discussion, but a very practical one. I told her how powerful it felt to literally melt away and find underneath a person from who others didn't recoil in revulsion.

My PCP (yes, the same guy that told me I was too fat to survive) asked if I needed a long-term inpatient facility to deal with the anorexia. This idea horrified me. Lynn understood better than almost anyone except Dr. Guterson that I had already done my eight-month stay in an inpatient unit and was not exactly well-served by the experience.

She said to me, 'Then think about thinking about eating.'

I didn't have many options. If eating meant not being sent away for another chunk of my life, I had to consider the food as a less evil choice. An equally unappetizing option was a feeding tube. I told her I was really scared and didn't know where to start. She told me that my question was a medical one. If I were willing to try, she'd pass the news on to Dr. Guterson and he'd take it from there. Her persuasion and caring won the day. I told her I'd try.

Over the coming days she worked slowly, patiently, and compassionately with me. We sat together with a small protein shake between us and she coached me, one sip at a time. I was up to three protein shakes in her presence. Not nearly enough by medical standards, but an improvement over days of fasting. Each time she left, after one of our sip sessions, she gave me a hug. Lynn was the only person, aside from Katie, who I ever let touch me. Her hugs reminded me that mercy and tenderness still existed in the world.

One particular day after one of our sip sessions, I watched as she made her way to the nursing unit and had a conversation with someone behind the glass. The unit was designed as four halls all passing the nursing unit, which acted as a hub. Two halls were occupied by patient rooms, the third was offices, and the fourth contained the recreation rooms, dining area, lounges, and treatment rooms. The nursing unit was not only the geographical hub, but also one of activity. Physicians, nurses, technicians, therapists, and random staff buzzed in and out of the glass enclosure at all hours of the day and night. Patients were not exactly welcome at the hub unless summoned.

I could hear the click as the auto-locked doors came to life. As Lynn approached the exit, I felt a pang of loneliness. She was free. I was still there. I decided to check out the lounge area. It was one of those rare times that I had been out of my room to socialize since admission, whenever that was. I needed to ask someone what the answer to that question was. I was desperate to know just how long I had been in the clutches of the alternate dimension. It was midday and other patients had pulled up plastic chairs and gathered around the televisions. I didn't care what was on and I didn't want to make pointless chatter, but I didn't want to be alone either.

The air-conditioning unit in the lounge must have been working overtime because I was shivering. It could have had something to do with the fact that I had no body fat and I was wearing a hospital gown the old me could never have fit into. An aide came up to me and greeted me warmly. She looked familiar, but I couldn't remember when I had met her or what her name was. She was a young African American woman, pretty, wearing scrubs with smiling cartoon characters on them. Her nametag read "Beth". She seemed genuinely pleased to see me out of my room. I liked her and asked her if I could sit next to her.

Curled up in one of the over-sized vinyl chairs, I felt welcomed. I found it weird to think that the old me would have filled up the whole chair and would have needed help to get up. The new me occupied a corner of the chair, my feet involuntarily dancing on the floor, and there was still room left for another person. Times had indeed changed.

Beth noticed me shivering as I sat in the chair. She said kindly, 'I'll bring you a blanket.' For some reason, her thoughtful gesture made me well up with unbidden tears. She put the blanket around me and asked if I was warmer. I choked out, 'Much.' She told me she was with me the night I'd ended up in restraints and was glad to see I was doing better.

'Yeah, Dr. Guterson's a genius.'

Beth laughed. 'Super nice, too.' Dr. Guterson had another fan besides me. I was sure we could form a club.

A male nurse approached me. His nametag read "Chuck" and he said he wanted to speak to me. We went into the empty recreation room and Chuck told me brusquely that I had been ordered two Ensure shakes for dinner. He kind of glared at me and said, 'You are expected to drink them. I'm not in the mood to play games with you.'

This guy brought back bad memories of Dr. X. I'd had no previous experience with Chuck and yet he seemed purposefully menacing. His voice oozed hostility and his body language spoke to me like he was about to lunge if I wasn't completely acquiescent. But, of course, I wasn't going to be completely compliant. I was still manic. I was impulsive, fidgety, quick to anger, and had boundless energy that would have me occasionally dancing in the halls. I was also still manic enough to be impervious to his antagonism. I rolled my eyes at him as he lectured me. I was ready to snarl that he couldn't make me drink anything and if he was so interested in getting the Ensure consumed, he could pour it down his own throat. I had gone from warm and safe to defiant and angry.

Chuck exited before I could rant at him. How dare he leave before I could eviscerate him? However, I remembered my promise to Lynn and by extension Dr. Guterson. I'd drink the damn Ensures and chuck the bottles at Chuck. I giggled, yelling, 'Food fight!' Now I was eagerly anticipating dinner and the image of Chuck drenched in Ensure.

*

Baby steps – I was healing in baby steps. Dr. Guterson came into my room for one of our daily morning chats. He and Lynn were the high points of my day, though I would have much preferred to see each of them in their cozy offices. He wanted to discuss my new medication regimen, as he'd rearranged my medications without my having noticed. He explained the changes to me: he'd increased my dose of Risperdal and he'd added Klonopin. Yes, the dreaded Klonopin was back. He assured me it was only until the manic episode was completely resolved. And there was another surprise: lithium.

I hadn't been on lithium since I had swallowed the whole bottle way back before I even knew Dr. Guterson.

I asked him about that. He wasn't convinced that there would be a problem re-administering the drug. He called lithium the "gold standard" for bipolar mania. He was keeping me on the Depakote, however. He told me the two were often used in combination as mood stabilizers. So, I picked up one permanent drug, had an increase in a second drug, kept two other drugs the same, and was temporarily taking a drug I hated. I accepted the fact that my medicine cabinet just got a bit fuller.

As he got out of his chair to leave, I had one more burning question for him. 'Dr. Guterson, time is so messed up in here for me. I have no idea how long I've been here or how long I spent living in the alternate universe. Can you tell me?'

He replied in a measured tone. 'You've been here four weeks. Three of those weeks you were severely manic. The mania is resolving with the new medications.'

I grasped neither the significance of the duration of my hospitalization nor understood that in spite of aggressive treatment, the mania still wasn't resolved. Instead I asked, 'When can I go home?'

Dr. Guterson stiffened a bit. 'Tova, you aren't ready. When you are, you, Lynn, and I will know it. You still aren't eating enough. You're still showing signs of mania. I need to be sure the new drug combination will be effective. I don't want you to have to go through an episode like this again.'

I felt chastened and guilt-ridden. 'I didn't cause this to happen, honestly.' I started to cry.

Dr. Guterson responded gently to my obvious misinterpretation. 'No, of course you didn't. We do need to try to understand why this episode happened, however. You haven't had a manic episode in almost 15 years. I don't have an answer to why yet, but we need to find one.'

I still felt guilty. 'Are you angry with me?' I asked in a childlike manner.

Dr. Guterson was completely puzzled by my question. 'Why would you ever think I'd be angry with you for becoming ill? I'm just very concerned that something else is causing this episode.'

I wiped away tears with the back of my hand.

'We'll figure it out,' he said gently. It'll be okay.'

He left then, and I continued to wallow in groundless guilt. *I've caused so much trouble for everyone,* I thought. I tried to shake off the shame.

*

Life fell into a predictable routine in the hospital. I saw Dr. Guterson every morning, Lynn every afternoon, and a surly Chuck far too often. Days flowed into weeks. Finally, the session with Dr. Guterson that I'd long sought after came He told me that he and Lynn thought I was ready to be discharged. I wasn't manic. I was adjusting to my medications. I had gained six pounds. The criteria for being released from my long hospitalization had been met. In total, I had been an inpatient for almost eight weeks. The only hospitalization I had ever had that was longer was my eight-month stay back in 1994.

I walked off the psychiatric ward a free woman, but not without trepidation. As much as I wanted to be free, I was scared. Two months is a long time to live isolated from the world. I would have to reintegrate into "normal" and I wasn't all that gifted at navigating life, even on my best days. Even scarier was my pending return to work. I had been placed on short-term disability while I was hospitalized. That necessitated Human Resources knowing the full nature of my illness. How could I ever walk back into work knowing that my secret was out?

I decided the answer was that I hold my head high, do my job well, answer questions without being defensive, and settle back into my routine quickly. It really was time for me to go back to work. Besides, I had a secret weapon. I had Team Tova. I knew I would be just fine.

*

Dr. Guterson and I were about to play medical detectives. The problem, as he saw it, was that I had a severe manic episode after being symptom-free for over a decade. We teased out that the only change – and it was a seismic one – that could have precipitated that degree of relapse was my gastric bypass surgery. Everyone we consulted, my GBS surgeon, my PCP, my endocrinologist, the rare journal article we could find related to the subject, all agreed that the surgery was most likely the precipitating cause for my vicious psychotic–manic episode, but no one had an exact idea of why. A number of theories were floated. One was that absorption changes that occur as a result of GBS may have interfered with medication absorption. Another theory was that hormone changes that occur in the body as a consequence of the surgery might have played a factor. A third theory was that my anorexia triggered the episode. There was a fourth factor that wasn't identified till much later.

I'd developed a rare complication to GBS. I had lost the ability to appropriately regulate my blood sugar. If I ate a meal with any kind of carbohydrate my blood sugar would spike. Not a little bit, but into severe diabetes range. Unlike a diabetic, my extreme highs would be followed by extreme lows. I could go from a meter reading of 450 to a meter reading of 40 within two or three hours, having done absolutely nothing to cause the plunge. Eventually my number would level off into a normal range on its own. However, this happened every time I ate a meal. To complicate matters further, we didn't know what the impact of my anorexia had on this phenomenon. There was a lot of medical data for Dr. Guterson to consider in order to create an effective treatment plan for me.

It took a year for medical science to catch up with my crazy biology. During that time, my concerns were ignored by one physician, minimized by another, and viewed as "impossible" by a third. My third endocrinologist saw my situation as a challenge, and worked in close collaboration with me and Dr. Guterson to develop an interdisciplinary treatment plan. Her first step was to confirm the spiking and crashing phenomena my glucose meter detected, by using a sophisticated blood sugar monitor that was inserted under my skin. The device took readings all day long, every seven minutes, for one week. After the data was downloaded and analyzed, the pattern that emerged was unmistakable.

Every time I ate there was a massive sugar spike. Two hours later there was a massive sugar crash. Another few hours later the sugar leveled out. She told me that this complication tended to emerge in patients two or more years after GBS surgery. It was rare and still poorly understood.

As far as pinning down the cause for my relapse, we had plenty of theories, some literature to support those theories, and actual data, but nailing the exact cause would remain elusive. Dr. Guterson, my endocrinologist and I decided to try an experiment to see if tightly controlling my sugar levels would impact my bipolar episodes. My endocrinologist, prescribed the solution to the glucose problem. We hypothesized that if we could control the spikes and crashes of my glucose levels, we could have an impact on my bipolar symptoms. A combination of careful medication dosing, symptom monitoring, and a stringent glucose management routine did significantly reduce the severity and frequency of the manic episodes. They weren't eliminated completely. I still had episodes of mania, but they were far less frequent and much less life-disrupting. We seemed to have found the solution to my devastating psychotic – manic episode.

Dr. Guterson and I, with help, had solved the case. As I considered my odyssey into the edges of modern medicine, I realized I had been co-opted into Team Tova. Dr. Guterson and Lynn had pulled off the impossible. I was not just active in my care; I had collaborated with my treatment team to solve a vexing mystery.

Lynn and Dr. Guterson managed to get me to own my recovery. Medication and monitoring were in Dr. Guterson's purview. Managing my glucose levels was mine and my endocrinologist's. If I didn't do my job, their jobs would be very difficult. I realized that we were all in this together.

CHAPTER 8

The chuck incident

In every relationship of any significant duration, external forces sometimes align to pull at the threads in the fabric of that bond. Such was the case with me and Dr. Guterson in the summer of 2013. In our 17 years together, we had weathered psychotic mania, brutal depressions, anorexia, severe trauma reactions, medical crises, and the ups and downs that came with my reentry into "normal" life. I was so comfortable and so secure in my relationship with him that I couldn't conceive of anything happening between us that would ever threaten that bond. I felt completely safe, cared about, and protected.

Then Chuck happened.

It was July. I was still struggling with the reemergence of active bipolar symptoms as a result of gastric bypass surgery complications. This particular summer, I'd also had a resurgence of traumatic childhood memories. I went where my psyche always goes when trauma meets bipolar disorder: the malevolent forces from the alternate dimension.

I refer to these creatures simply as THEM. In my mind, THEY must always remain nameless because the mere mention of their identity still returns me to places where childhood dwells. As always, I was obsessed with fighting THEM and had come to believe that my food and medications had been contaminated by these all-powerful forces. I knew if I ate contaminated food or took contaminated medication, I would forever be their servant. I feared for the safety of everyone I loved and strangers in lands oceans away. Every plane crash, tornado, hurricane, and wild fire was THEIR evil plot. I, as always, was the Earth's only hope. If I fell to their influence, mankind was lost. I feared that the body count across the world would mount that summer if I could not fight THEM. My first priority was not allowing myself to be converted into one of their minions. I stopped taking my medication. THEY, I was certain, were tampering with the bottles. Everything escalated from that choice.

Dr. Guterson, during our routine bimonthly appointment, noticed immediately the all-too-familiar pattern. He once again admitted me to the hospital directly from his office. It had been almost exactly a year since my previous hospitalization, precipitated also by THEM. My resolve to not have my brain co-opted didn't change just because my geographic location had. I still steadfastly refused to be medicated, and my downward spiral accelerated. No one seemed to understand that I was saving lives by not becoming one of THEIR acolytes. I tried to explain to everyone and anyone who tried to medicate me that I was acting heroically. I was resolute that there would be no plane crash in the Himalayas if I just held firm.

Because I was willfully unmedicated and wildly symptomatic, a mental health aide was assigned to me around the clock. I must have talked endlessly about THEM because I was so desperate for someone to understand and agree with me. Dr. Guterson was carefully neutral when it came to my war with the alternate dimensional forces. He was quite firm that the best option for relieving my suffering was taking my medication. But I wasn't worried about *my* suffering. I was worried about what THEY would inflict on everyone else ... including him, if I relented.

One shift of nurses after another brought me medication that I refused to take. And then entered Chuck. He was middle-aged, medium build, with salt and pepper hair. His demeanor toward me during past admissions had always been surly, even bordering on hostile. At this particular admission, he exploded. His diatribe shattered my already tenuous grasp on reality.

'Take these meds NOW. I'm sick of your games,' Chuck bellowed.

'I can't, don't you understand? I can't!' I said, quivering in terror.

He snarled, 'People are tired of your bull crap and no one believes a word you say.'

I recoiled from him, petrified. THEY were speaking through Chuck now. I was sure of it.

With derision dripping from his voice, Chuck sneered. 'Your story is the dumbest thing I've ever heard. You must have gotten that from some TV show or a movie because no one would say something that ridiculous.'

Now I was absolutely certain that Chuck had become THEIR agent and was out to destroy me. I curled into a fetal position on my bed. 'Please stop,' I begged. 'Please. You are giving THEM power. Please. Just stop.'

Chuck continued his frontal assault, but I couldn't hear him anymore. I was racked in hysterical sobs, trembling, and in mortal combat with the ENEMY. I continued to plead with him to stop and go away.

Chuck started to sound like the adults in the *Peanuts* cartoons to me. All I heard was his ridicule and contempt, not his words. He continued to lash out at me in fury for what seemed like an eternity. When he either realized that I was impenetrable or he had exhausted his need for brutality, he left my room.

I lay collapsed in a heap on my bed, heaving uncontrollably, unable to catch my breath. The aide in the room tried to soothe me.

She told me he shouldn't have treated me like that. I was so absolutely destroyed that I couldn't acknowledge her. Moments later, I felt someone sit on my bed right next to me and a hand lay on my back. I looked up. It was Lynn. As best I could, I explained what happened between Chuck and me. Thank goodness the aide was a witness to the whole ordeal, because no one would have taken my word for it. I continued to sob. Lynn cradled my head and rubbed my back. It was like she knew I was an infant in need of tender human touch in order to breathe.

I heard a second voice. It was Dr. Guterson. Lynn left me for a moment to speak to him. I returned to my wrenching sobs and never heard a word the two of them shared. When he left the room, she returned to me. Lynn continued to cradle and soothe me until my sobs subsided. I looked at Lynn and whispered, 'Will Dr. Guterson fix it?'

'I'll bet he does,' she responded in her gentle and comforting tone. I leaned my head on her shoulder. I believed he would also.

The remainder of my hospitalization became a cat and mouse game with Chuck. When I caught a glimpse of him, I'd dive into whatever room was nearest to me. I ducked into other patients' rooms, into treatment rooms, even under tables and behind couches. I wasn't just frightened of him; I was downright phobic. Every morning I would hold my stomach, studying the nursing assignment board and praying I wasn't on his rotation. I couldn't eat. I couldn't sleep. It was only because of Lynn that I began to swallow my medication again. A few days after Chuck's assault, Lynn sat me down.

Her gaze was compassionate but determined. 'Do you trust Dr. Guterson and me?' she asked.

With absolute childlike faith, I answered, 'With every ounce of me.'

'Then trust us right now. Please take your medication. I promise you that Dr. Guterson and I – the forces of good – cannot be turned by the forces of darkness.'

I was completely stunned by her assertion. 'Then I'm not the only one fighting THEIR evil?'

She answered simply. 'Nope.'

I sat for a few minutes trying to digest this revelation. Lynn and Dr. Guterson were in this battle against THEM with me? Amazed, I asked the question again, just in case. 'I don't have to fight THEM alone?'

Lynn studied my confused face intently. 'Never again.'

I instinctively believed her and was ready at that moment to take a leap of faith. I took a deep breath and clenched my hands. 'Okay,' I answered. 'For the forces of good, I'll try.'

From that moment on, I took my medication. I believed Lynn and Dr. Guterson were powerful allies against THEIR plans. *The three of us could certainly stop plane crashes,* I mused.

As the medications took effect, I slowly returned, yet again, from the grips of the alternate dimension. However, Chuck happened to reign supreme in this dimension.

*

I began to notice a pattern in my conversations with Dr. Guterson. In our daily morning chats, he would not address my abuse at the hands of Chuck. He simply wouldn't discuss it. I chalked it up to the fact that I was still in the hospital and it probably wasn't a good place to discuss a staff member. I decided that I could be patient until we were in the safety of his office.

In the meantime, I did notice that Chuck was never my nurse again. Lynn and I believed the severity of the trauma he inflicted on me made the hospital a very dangerous place to be in, and Dr. Guterson couldn't be there around the clock to protect me. The only solution was to discharge me early, but there was no way I was ready.

However, I knew I'd *never* be ready with Chuck stalking the halls. At least if I wasn't constantly running into him, maybe the trauma would have time to resolve. I had Dr. Guterson and Lynn to help me put the pieces back together. After days of my badgering and piteous pleading, I finally got Dr. Guterson to reluctantly discharge me. I had entered the hospital a victim of my illnesses. I walked out of the hospital a victim of staff abuse.

*

With both anticipation and dread, I met with Dr. Guterson only days after discharge. I thought now he'd be free to talk about Chuck's assault. I sat down in the familiar upholstered chair and watched him behind his desk. I brought up the subject of Chuck.

Dr. Guterson looked at me with a completely inscrutable look on his face. After all our years together, I had become expert at reading his facial expressions, vocal inflections, body language, and demeanor. If I wasn't wildly manic or psychotic, I could almost predict what he was thinking or might say. This look was one that I had never seen before, and it worried me.

I took a different approach. I told him Lynn and I had discussed me writing a letter to the senior hospital administration, detailing Chuck's mistreatment and how it had affected me. Dr. Guterson acknowledged that the idea was a good one and he even provided me with the names of people I should notify. *Okay,* I thought to myself. *He's on board with my letter of grievance. But he still doesn't want to talk about it in depth. Maybe there's a reason he still can't talk about it.*

The letter I crafted began by praising the care I had received at their hospital over the years. I mentioned specific staff members who went above and beyond the call of duty on my behalf during this last admission. Then I described in detail the trauma Chuck inflicted on me. I concluded my letter the following way:

I am one of the lucky ones. I have Dr. Guterson and my psychologist Lynn to help me make sense of being abused by someone who had a duty to help me when I was desperately ill. There are patients at your hospital who do not have the excellent clinical support I have. What happens to those extremely vulnerable people if Chuck does to them what he did to me?

I shared my letter with Lynn. She said it was "effectively and professionally written".

At my next session with Dr. Guterson, I prepared to share the letter with him. We had the most confounding conversation. I said, 'I wrote the letter informing the senior hospital administration about Chuck's assault on me. I'd like to read it to you.'

Dr. Guterson looked at me with that inscrutable expression again, and answered with disinterest. 'No, that's okay. I trust you. I'm sure it's fine.'

Utterly stunned by both his words and demeanor, I asked again, 'You don't want to hear what I've written about Chuck to hospital administration?'

Looking down at my file and scribbling notes, he responded absently, 'It's not necessary.'

I felt like I had been punched in the gut. Never, from my very earliest essays, had Dr. Guterson ever refused to read something I had written. Never in a million years could I have ever believed that he would pick this piece of writing to suddenly "trust me". Something was wrong – very, very, wrong. I didn't even feel hurt. I felt tossed into a vortex of uncertainty and bewilderment.

There had to be some reason Dr. Guterson absolutely refused, in spite of numerous requests and pleas by me, to talk about the psychological violence I lived through under his care on his unit. Lynn suggested it might be a Human Resources issue, and he had to stay neutral until a plan concerning Chuck was made. That seemed plausible to me, but it didn't explain the fact that he wouldn't even discuss how I was doing after the fact. Never once did he ask me how I was coping with this recent trauma. All of this was so un-him.

I swallowed hard and tried to absorb the thought that he truly did not care about what I had endured. A sickening thought came into my consciousness: what if the real answer was that Chuck was

Dr. Guterson's colleague, maybe friend? What if, when it came right down to a choice of protecting me or protecting his colleague, he chose his colleague? A wave of nausea rose up from my gut. Could it be that when it came right down to it, he wasn't going to risk a relationship with someone he worked with to defend me? Was I unworthy of protection if it meant it might cost him something?

From there, I made a horrifying connection. The nameless, faceless physicians from my childhood, the ones that saw the aftermath of trauma but didn't get involved, might provide the clue to Dr. Guterson's behavior.

On that afternoon in my hospital room, when Lynn and I were confident Dr. Guterson would shield me, maybe he'd just walked away because he didn't want to get involved. Maybe he was just biding his time, hoping the whole incident would go away. In all our years together, he never had to intervene for me because I was being actively abused. But when presented with that unprecedented moment, maybe he chose to abandon me because it was easier.

I didn't know for sure that any of my fears were based on fact, but as his steadfast refusal to even enquire about how I was doing continued, I was left with little else. Lynn and I discussed ad nauseam every angle of his seeming coldness. She had no counterargument. She just didn't know and I was flung downward into an emotional spiral where everything I thought I knew and could trust in my therapeutic relationship with him was now in doubt.

After weeks of effort trying to break through his wall, I stopped trying. I dropped back to a defensive and mistrustful position. I looked on him with suspicion and trepidation. I would leave his office wondering who it was that I'd been pouring my soul out to all these years. Who was this person to who I had entrusted my sanity, sometimes my life? Could he really be someone that had just turned a blind eye when I was being actively ill-treated? My head said impossible. My intuition said maybe. My toddler's heart was broken.

Lynn became my oracle of wisdom and sanity. We teased this crisis out in every possible way but we could not resolve it because Dr. Guterson refused to talk. So, we worked around him. For things I would normally have gone to him with, I went to Lynn. I let her find the answers and bring them back to me. Appointments with Dr. Guterson changed profoundly. I answered what was asked of me. I hid information. I kept spontaneous conversation about my illnesses to a minimum. I just didn't feel safe anymore in his presence. The gut-wrenchingly painful truth was that he never even noticed the change in our communication. Could I have possibly been that inconsequential to him?

*

Lynn's office has a comfy tan leather couch. I love to kick my shoes off and snuggle right into it. What is it with psychologists and snuggly couches?

Anyway, this one particular day, I got comfortable on Lynn's couch, sipped my tea, and waited for her. She came in looking somber, not her normal expression. I jovially asked her what was up. She gave me an answer I never expected.

In a subdued voice, she said to me, 'Dr. Guterson's dad passed away yesterday. I didn't want you to hear it out in the community, especially given the complexity of your situation with him right now. I wanted to tell you myself.'

I sat in silence for a minute. Then I asked her how he was. 'He's with family,' she said. I wanted to do something for him, anything that might bring some comfort. I asked Lynn if I wrote him a condolence letter, would she get it to him. She said absolutely.

At home, I sat in front of my notepad for over an hour, trying to parse out the exact words that would express my sympathy and sorrow at his loss. I wrote and rewrote. I was awash in the most confusing and tangled mix of feelings imaginable. The immediate goal was offering compassion and comfort to a man who, up until several months ago, had been my source of compassion and comfort. Underneath that layer was the vortex of emotional chaos Chuck had wrought in my life. At the basement level dwelled this toddler inside me, terrified that the relationship she had come to trust and depend on for so long might be permanently fractured.

As I wrote my condolence note, I wept for all the losses. I wept for his loss, the loss of my trust, and the loss of the safety Chuck robbed from me. I sent the letter to Lynn. She told me it was perfect and she would make sure Dr. Guterson received it. I knew I had done all I could do and was appropriate for me to do for him. But it didn't seem like enough.

I had no way of knowing that I was falling into what would become the deepest bipolar depression in Lynn's and my experience together, and I would have to endure it without Dr. Guterson's wise clinical counsel. I was also about to travel to my childhood home, Boston – or, as I thought of it, "the abyss". The combination would prove to be nearly lethal.

CHAPTER 9

The abyss

I wedged my small frame between two metal-armed chairs in Lynn's waiting room. Sinking to the floor, I pulled my knees to my chest and buried my head in my hands. Tears streamed down my face. Not wails or sobs, just the gentle flow of teardrops. Lynn tried to get my attention in order to usher me into her office. I never looked up. She kneeled softly down in front of me, touched my shoulder, and invited me in. Just like a lost toddler, I followed the grown-up. I made it into her office, sunk to the floor next to her comfy couch, and lowered my head. My dark hair fell in my face and again soft tears streamed down my cheeks.

Lynn and her tiny 62-year-old frame sat cross-legged just inches in front of me. She leaned forward to touch my hair and I laid my head on her shoulder. The stream of tears became a torrent. I started shaking. She knew it was depression. It was Dr. Guterson. I was suffering the grief of someone who believed a sacred trust had been violated. Lynn stroked my hair, tenderly trying to soothe my anguish, and let me weep.

When I finally spoke, it was to remind her that I was heading to Boston in two days for a three-day medical conference. This was the first professional conference I had attended in almost 20 years. I needed to go, both because it was a professional obligation and because it would have felt like a devastating failure to let my illness interfere with that obligation. Lynn noted with concern that this wasn't a good time for me to be going anywhere, least of all Boston.

*

I grew up in the city of Boston. There isn't a single landmark in that historic city that doesn't have some childhood memory attached to it. Fenway Park, the Boston Aquarium, Faneuil Hall, Boston Science Center, Harvard Square, the list goes on. My tortured childhood and young adulthood were inextricably bound up in these iconic places, and as a result, I hadn't laid eyes on the city in almost ten years.

Now, in my most fragile state of recent memory, I was returning to the scene of the crime. How were Lynn and I going to make it possible for me to survive this trip still whole? We arranged for phone sessions and text check-ins. She said she'd check her text messages between appointments and respond when she could. I looked down at my hands. They were trembling uncontrollably. She didn't know what to make of it – trauma, medication, something else, she didn't know. We decided to see if maybe the tremors would resolve spontaneously. There was no mention of Dr. Guterson. It was probably the first time in months he wasn't a discussion topic.

The bell rang in her office; Lynn's next client had arrived. I knew I needed to go and pack for Boston. She reached out for our usual post-session hug, and it was just a little bit longer and a little bit tighter. I was on my own now.

*

As the airplane circled Logan International Airport, I could feel my stomach knot up. The skyline had changed but Boston Harbor was the same. I watched the tiny islands that dotted the Bay come into focus and grow as we landed. When we hit the tarmac, my first thought was, *I'm home.* Nathan, a colleague and good friend of mine, was also on my flight. The two of us made our way to baggage claim – no easy feat in Logan – and we waited for the others in our department.

My hand tremors had been continuous since I had left Lynn's office. I tried to hide them under my coat.

Nathan knew I had bipolar disorder and he'd had a long research career studying psychotropic medication. 'Medication related?' he asked.

'I don't know,' I replied. 'They started two days ago.'

Looking concerned, he said, 'You should call Dr. Guterson.'

I made noises like that was a good idea, knowing full well I would ignore his counsel. We met up with the rest of our party and our group boarded the hotel shuttle. I watched as the city I knew the bowels of passed by me. I saw the USS Constitution sitting in the harbor. I looked at all the new construction that melded familiar with unfamiliar. The trip was disorientating. Boston was as it always had been for almost 400 years, and yet it had changed in profound, unrecognizable ways. Or maybe, I thought, I was the one who had changed in unrecognizable ways. Either way, I couldn't take it in. The tears flowed again.

The hotel we stayed in was in the Back Bay area. As everyone went to check-in, I patiently waited my turn. An overly vivacious hotel receptionist asked for my name and reservation number. I told her I was Tova Feinman and then handed her my reservation confirmation form. As she searched for my reservation in the computer, a look of panic came over her face. She looked up at me, embarrassed, and said, 'Mrs. Feinman, I don't have a reservation for you. Let me get my manager. Please have a seat in the lobby. I'll get back to you.' My instant thought was that I was now a homeless toddler in a city that wasn't very nice to toddlers.

I sat on a red velvet antique couch. It was both stunning – with its brass inlay, mahogany frame, and fanned headboard – and uncomfortable, because the seat was lumpy. I wanted Lynn's leather couch. I wanted Lynn. I shot her a text as I sat there. As I waited for a response, those darned tears started to flow again. I was already hiding my hands, and now I had to hide my face.

The manager approached me, apologized profusely for the reservation snafu, and said they had made a new reservation for me. This one upgraded me to a luxury suite on the 22nd floor. In addition, the hotel gave me a voucher for a complimentary breakfast or lunch in one of their multiple restaurants, my choice. I didn't have the heart to tell them that I kept kosher and couldn't eat in their restaurants, but I knew Nathan would appreciate the voucher so at least it wouldn't go to waste. The word "luxury" made me nervous, but the hotel had to do significant negotiating with my employer to smooth over the reservation error. It was best that I didn't fuss. My text message system pinged with a response from Lynn.

My luxury hotel suite was a palace. It was not the place for a former Peace Corps volunteer. In the large living room, there was an enormous flat screen television, brass and crystal light fixtures, a couch, and a set of overstuffed chairs that they must have commissioned from the artisans at the Harvard museums. There was a roll top antique oak desk, should I have felt the urge to write in the style of John Adams, and a carved oak and glass coffee table with matching end tables.

I felt like the maid. *That's why they put me here,* I thought. *To clean.* The real occupant was due any time. I knew I was both unworthy of the opulence and guilty for the indulgence. The bedroom also had a large flat screen TV. The overstuffed chairs were covered in cream-colored satin and the bed was king-sized with a cream and floral embroidered down comforter.

As I tried to reposition the comforter on the bed – it was off center – I realized I couldn't get it to budge. It weighed so much I literally could not get it to move. *There must be a lot of naked geese running around Boston because of this comforter,* I thought. I wondered how many hotel employees it took to make the bed with this thing weighing down on it. All this was a far cry from my days as a Peace Corps volunteer, sleeping on a straw mat in a mud hut.

I might have found the humor in that juxtaposition at a different point in time, but in that moment, the opulence only served to make me feel unworthy and ashamed.

Despite the extravagance of the room, to me, the most alluring features of this palace were the floor-to-ceiling smoked glass windows that spanned the entire east side of the room. I stood at the window in the living room, mesmerized by the tiny match-box-sized cars and the Polly Pocket-sized people that seemed to move at a sloth's pace 22 stories below. I didn't look out at the skyline, or contemplate the glorious sunrises I'd be privy to. I was transfixed by just how far down street level was.

My trance was broken by the ringing of my hotel suite phone. It was my Director, Nancy. She said the department was getting together for dinner at one of the Back Bay's trendy French Bistros, and she invited me to join them.

That was a dilemma. I kept kosher so I couldn't eat snail's tails or whatever crazy dish was being concocted in the kitchens around me. I was terrified that the isolation that had already swallowed me up would be magnified by my religious observance. At that moment, everything I did made me feel like an alien to the remainder of the human race.

To add to my misery, I couldn't make coherent conversation without the fear of an unbidden stream of tears erupting. However, I was here to work. I was being paid to be here. I must have paused too long because Nancy asked if I was still on the phone. After making my apologies, I told her I'd enjoy spending time with the department but I could only order diet soda. Sounding a bit peeved, she responded I was still welcome to join them.

The French Bistro was just as you would expect a trendy Boston dining hotspot to be, even on a Wednesday night. Stylishly dressed patrons queued up at the restaurant's stained glass double doors. The wait staff, dressed in smart tuxedo-like uniforms, attentively saw to the dining tastes of every guest. The wine list had its own separate leather-bound menu and went on for pages. Many of the selections had no price listing.

My colleagues ordered unpronounceable French dishes, glasses of wine, and delicate pastries for dessert. I ordered a diet soda, just like I had said I would. Despite my fears of feeling ostracized, no one made a comment about my dietary choice. I kept my severely trembling hands hidden in my lap and drank my diet soda with a straw.

Everything seemed to be going fine until the dinner conversation turned to family traditions, heirlooms, cute childhood memories, and the escapades of adult siblings. I sank back into silence. There was nothing I could contribute to this conversation that wouldn't make me feel like I was being knifed in my stomach. I made appropriate nods and asked questions in response to other people's stories. Then one of my colleagues asked me directly for a funny childhood story. I looked out the window, pretending I hadn't heard her. I was at the bottom of the abyss, Boston, and there were no amusing stories to be found here. I lamely said that I had a boring life compared to hers and I'd rather hear about her vacations in Canada. The table fell silent. I looked over to Nathan, pleading for help. He gave me a reassuring nod and began to regale us all with witty Little League baseball stories. Although the group was listening to Nathan, they were eyeing me. My tears might as well have been glowing neon green.

Back at the palace I had been given as my room, I stood again at the window, transfixed by the points of light emanating from the street and buildings so far below. The pinpricks of light that illuminated the street's blackness looked like stars that had fallen to Earth by mistake. I had this overpowering urge to yell to them, 'Go back, nothing good can happen if you stay here!'

I collapsed on the king-sized bed. It swallowed me up, it was so plush. I wept tears of grief, shame, embarrassment, and hopelessness. I heard my cell phone ring through the haze; it was Lynn. I answered it, weeping yet again. At the end of our conversation – which consisted of me sobbing and her trying to soothe me – I told her that I wished I could kill myself and have everything be over. She coached me through taking Dr. Guterson's medication cocktail, and verbally tucked me into bed. She made me promise I would call her before I did anything, even if it was 2am. I promised.

As I lay under the goose down comforter, I had the sensation that the comforter was dirt and I was being buried alive. I drifted off into a nightmare-laced sleep.

*

The morning sunrise took on a gray hue from my tinted palace window, matching the view from my inner window as well. I choked down a kosher bagel and cream cheese, and washed it down with British-style tea. I glued myself together as best I could, and texted Lynn that I was due to attend an early morning lecture, but all I wanted to really do was watch the doll house people and their Lego vehicles crawl far below me. She told me to stay in touch and she'd text me between appointments.

All I had to hang on to at that moment were text messages with Lynn. We were supposed to turn our cell phones off during the workshops, but I kept mine on vibrate. My tremors were just as bad as they had been on Monday afternoon in Lynn's office, which meant I now faced a practical problem. I couldn't hold a pen and take notes. My hands had become essentially useless. There was no way for me to record ideas, thoughts or questions as I sat in lectures and workshops. I would have to do everything from memory. Unfortunately, my head was crammed full of images from my palace window. There was absolutely no room left for medical science in my brain.

I'd have to figure out a way to grasp the pen so that it stabilized my hand. Making a fist around the pen, just like a baby would, I attempted to spell my name. The scribble was almost illegible, but it was all I had. I got through the morning workshops by taking crudely scratched notes. Between the incessant tremors and my odd grasp on the pen, my hand cramped up. It became difficult to uncurl, painful.

Lunch was next on the schedule.

My department gathered together in the Grand Ballroom, converted into a dining room, where the lunch provided by the conference would be served. I received my kosher meal, triple-wrapped in plastic with utensils inside and carefully sealed. At first, I hid my hands in my lap and tried to figure out how I was going to eat. I fumbled with the wrapping, dropped the container a number of times, and the humiliation exploded inside me. Nathan, who was sitting next to me, whispered, 'A lot of these new sealed containers are tough to open. I can slice the plastic wrap with my pocket knife, would that help?'

I managed to nod, and within seconds he had sliced open the plastic, careful to not touch any of the food or utensils. I mouthed, 'Thank you.'

Nathan mouthed back at me, 'No problem.' As I got up to leave, he followed me out. Concerned, he asked, 'Did you call Dr. Guterson?'

'Not yet,' I confessed.

He looked alarmed. 'Tova, call him.'

'There is nothing he can do,' I snapped back, defensively. 'I'm 800 miles away. I'm sorry I'm such a pain.' I was really crying at that point.

With an expression of compassion on his face, he said, 'Why don't you sit the afternoon sessions out? I'll tell Nancy you got food poisoning from all the French food you didn't eat last night.'

I shook my head at him, but he managed to get me to stop crying. I returned to my palace.

*

My humiliation was complete. Nathan had to come to my rescue. We were friends but not so close that I could be comfortable with being that vulnerable in front of him. I stared out the window again, looking down at the Little Tykes people below. Instead of just staring out this time, I put my hands on the glass. The bitter New England chill seeped through.

I couldn't help but think that the only thing separating me from the pavement was this thick wall of glass. *Glass can be broken.* My mood brightened. First, I pushed on the glass, and then I started pounding on it like I was trapped inside the palace. An eerie calm settled over me. I went to the far end of the living room and I flung myself like a projectile at that window. The glass rebuffed me. I slid down the window to the floor, panting, but still determined. Something heavy would break the glass, I reasoned, and then I would be free.

The carved oak and glass end table caught my eye. It was heavy. I dragged it to the window. As I struggled to lift it, my phone began to vibrate on the bed. There was a text message waiting for me, probably from Lynn. My destruction was almost complete. The humiliation caused by my useless hands and the tears that would not stop, the gilded cage I was trapped in, the entire city of Boston, and a Marianas Trench of a depression, all conspired against me.

And right at the center of the vortex was the corroding and insidious unknown about Dr. Guterson and the Chuck Incident. Was the once bedrock-solid relationship I had come to depend on essentially over? Was it now permanently altered into something frosty and callous?

I received another text message from Lynn, which made three in less than half an hour. Decision time: the window or Lynn's insistent messages. I picked up my phone and typed, "Desperate." In minutes, the phone rang. In her exquisitely familiar therapeutic voice, Lynn said, 'What's doing, honey?'

In that phone call, I spilled my guts. I told her about the window, every moment of shame, the time warp Boston was for me, the depth of my depression, and the wrenching fear that there was no repair for Dr. Guterson's and my relationship.

Because Lynn is, at her core, a very pragmatic therapist, she listened and then made a practical plan.

- **Step one:** stay out of my room except to sleep.

- **Step two:** go to every workshop, even if I absorb nothing.

- **Step three:** do not spend time in the city. Stay only in the hotel.

- **Step four:** spend time in one of the hotel restaurants drinking tea and writing down, as best my hands will allow, what I am feeling about Dr. Guterson and Boston. Include everything.

- **Step five:** message her whenever I want and she will answer.

I did as she asked and returned to the conference. I ran into Nathan and apologized. He matter-of-factly said I was no problem, and we sat together at the next lecture. He whispered that he'd take notes for both of us. I remember thinking, *if he weren't happily married and very Catholic …* I could feel the darkness of the last hours receding from my consciousness because of his kindness.

*

At one of the conference computer terminals, I checked their website after my last lecture. I wanted to see if there were any evening activities scheduled in the hotel. I needed something to do. I saw an intriguing notification on the conference website. There was to be minyan at 6pm every evening of the conference. It stressed that all Jews – Reform, Conservative, and Orthodox – were welcome. As an observant Jewish woman, the thought of going to weekday evening minyan seemed inappropriate. The obligation for thrice daily prayer falls to men. We women are seen as being more naturally connected to G-d, so the obligation does not apply to us. However, I didn't feel all that connected to G-d at that moment, so on Thursday evening I went.

There were both men and women in kipahs, and as a cross-section of Jewish diversity, it was interesting. Men wear kipahs as an outward sign of their obedience to G-d. Again, because of our special status, women do not have the same obligation. But I didn't go to minyan to compare and contrast traditional and non-traditional Judaism. I went to pray.

I watched as the genders separated themselves. The observant men pulled the room partition out in order to have privacy. There was a handout with evening prayers printed in Hebrew and English. I found a quiet corner of the room on the opposite side of the partition from the men, where I could have privacy and pray. The melodic voices of the men davening brought me great solace. At the conclusion of the evening, I noticed there were a few copies of the Psalms available. I picked up a copy and I thought of Dr. Guterson. *Maybe the wisdom contained in the Psalms might bring both of us comfort in our losses.*

I began at Psalm 1 and I soaked in one at a time until the chairs were being put back and the lights were being shut off. I took the copy of Psalms, telling myself I was only borrowing it. I knew that the Sabbath (Shabbos) began at sundown on Friday, the next evening. I also knew that there would be minyan to welcome in the Shabbos, but I had no other plan for the day of rest. Now, however, I had Psalms and hope.

That Saturday, I stayed in my room reading and praying – for Dr. Guterson in his loss, and me in mine. I'd brought a copy of the Bible with me from home and located where we had left off in Synagogue the previous Shabbos. I studied, prayed, ate fruit and cheese, and curled up on my bed and wept. At nightfall, I emerged from my room to eat an actual meal.

Some of my group had left for home before I emerged from my Shabbos observance. Nathan, for example, had gone to spend an overnight with family. My flight wasn't until 11am Sunday morning. I resumed following Lynn's instructions and took up residence at the chic coffee bar in the hotel lobby. They had tea as well. Any place that serves tea is a safe place for me.

The grief was back; bottomless, impenetrable, and smothering. Following Lynn's instructions, I wrote a letter to G-d. I wrote about hating Boston and all the memories it held, but mostly I begged Him for the wisdom to understand what had gone wrong between Dr. Guterson and me. As I sipped my plum tea and ate kosher biscotti, emptiness consumed me. There would be no resolution so long as I stayed in Boston. I needed to return home to the city where Katie was born and my grown-up life was based. Boston was the toddler's city. I belonged somewhere else.

As I flew out the following morning, I watched as the tiny islands of the Bay disappeared from sight. I was going home to Katie, Lynn, Dr. Guterson, and uncertainty.

CHAPTER 10

The road to

REPAIRING THE BOND

I settled into my taxi for the 40-minute drive home from the airport. The vehicle smelled of stale heat, French fries, and lingering perfume. As the cab crossed through the main overpass, the sundrenched skyline of the city's steel and glass buildings gleamed. They were bathed in gold and their sparkle was almost blinding.

For anyone who hasn't been to Chicago, that first visual blast of the coliseum-like sports stadia and iconic corporate logos displayed on towering edifices can be humbling. Even in my dark depression, this sun-splashed splendor of the city's profile felt welcoming. The important people in my life were here: Katie, Lynn, and yes, Dr. Guterson. I had no answers for the gut-wrenching events of the previous months, but at least we shared geography once again. I was consoled by that.

When I arrived at my house, I dumped my collection of luggage, conference tote bag, and purse in the middle of the living room floor. My cats Pumpkin, a moose of an orange tabby, and Rosebud, a delicate empress calico, greeted me. They looked well – cared for and only mildly peeved that they had been left with the cat-sitter for four days. I took inventory of the house. It was in complete disarray. I had no energy to even pick up the TV remote that had been knocked on the floor. I wondered to myself what the cats had been watching while I was gone – pay-per-view or *Animal Planet?* I'd know when the cable bill came. I went to the kitchen and put the tea kettle on. I had my priorities. I needed tea. Everything else could wait.

I flopped down on my well-worn couch and breathed a sigh of relief that I was no longer trapped at the palace in my Boston hotel. The act of kicking off my shoes and sipping my tea, even with my still trembling hands, helped me feel more oriented. As the hours drifted by, the tears started to flow, again. Yes, I was where I belonged, but a gaping wound that needed bandaging remained. I had no clue how to begin the suturing. A single tear became a torrent.

The dawning realization that I was emotionally, spiritually, and physically incapable of coping with this chasm that had developed in my relationship with Dr. Guterson turned my thoughts to my spiritual mentor of many years, Rabbi Menachem. What would he advise I do? I'd leaned heavily on Lynn these past few months. I felt I owed her a break. I needed fresh insight.

The merely obvious answer came to me: *ask him.* I needed him now. I needed him to help me begin to knit the frayed fibers of Dr. Guterson's and my relationship back together. Because I had shared so much with my rabbi over the years about Dr. Guterson's and my relationship, he possessed special insight. His counsel would provide much needed wisdom.

*

When I finally made contact, I dumped the contents of my anguish at his feet. He paused for a minute after I was done, and then said, 'Dr. Guterson has a lot more to teach you. I don't see this relationship as irreparably damaged.' Then he gave me very specific advice. He told me to write Dr. Guterson a letter. Not just any letter, but a letter in which I poured my grief, hurt, confusion, anger, and panic onto its pages. He admonished me not to edit it, but to send it exactly as it spontaneously flowed from me. It's my habit to edit my writing to death, and yet I was being instructed to send probably the most crucial essay I had ever composed, completely raw. That scared me. What if it wasn't good enough?

When I expressed trepidation, he simply said, 'Don't judge your words. Trust them.' Then he very pointedly told me to have no expectations on how the letter would be received or what kind of response Dr. Guterson might give. Rabbi Menachem said I needed to let Dr. Guterson grapple with my letter in his own time and in his own way. He said, 'Don't assume rebuff. Don't assume acceptance. In fact, don't assume anything at all.' Most importantly, he told me to be patient.

When we finished speaking, I didn't feel confident that I could do as he asked. Nonetheless, the instructions came from Rabbi Menachem, so of course I would follow them. They were specific, pointed, and clear. In my deeply depressed state, they were all my imploded brain could grasp. His instructions were almost like advice Dr. Guterson might give me in a delicate psychiatric moment.

I followed his guidance exactly. There were times when my written words were those of the forsaken toddler from Boston. There were times when they were the sentiments of the betrayed teenager from my high school days. Sometimes I would beseech for understanding, but otherwise there was no pattern to what I wrote, no coherent theme. The letter rambled, got lost in its own expressions of despair and anguish.

However, as I was told to, I did not edit it. I did not judge it. I also had no confidence that this exercise would help the situation. I did exactly as Rabbi Menachem instructed anyway. After the essay was composed, I sent it as an attachment in an email to Lynn. I made the unusual request that she not read it. I told her I was following Rabbi Menachem's instructions. This letter was from me to Dr. Guterson only. Lynn wrote back that she totally understood and she forwarded the letter unopened. Now I just needed patience.

*

My post-Boston appointment with Dr. Guterson seemed to take forever to arrive. I had heard nothing from him since the forwarding of my email. Just as I began chewing myself alive with "what ifs", I'd remember Rabbi Menachem's insistence that I have no expectations. That was a lot harder to do than it was to hear. I made the decision to not bring the letter up at my appointment. I'd let Dr. Guterson do that. Didn't my rabbi say to let him respond in his own way and in his own time? To ask would be to force the issue, and that wasn't part of the agreement. So I prepared for my appointment by not preparing. This was truly a first in our relationship, as normally, I'd have a mental outline ready. As the appointment time on Wednesday evening approached, I did what I had always done for so many years: I went to see him.

I briefly greeted Mary. She seemed like she wanted to chat, but I couldn't find casual words for the normal small talk. I sat in the waiting room I had memorized over the years: his impressionist paintings and medical license hung on the walls, the boring magazines on his end tables, and Mary behind the glass. I soaked in its comfort. I could hear his inner office door open and then the sound of muffled voices. I sucked in my breath, clenched my still trembling hands, closed my eyes, and prayed for G-d's help. This little ritual calmed me. Dr. Guterson poked his head around the corner of the waiting room and greeted me in his usual casual and friendly manner. His tone was reassuringly recognizable. I sat across the desk from him. He had my voluminous file open and he was reading something. I said nothing.

He finally looked up at me and, with concern, said, 'It sounds like Boston was pretty rough.'

I almost lost it in a flood of tears, but I composed myself. 'It was brutal.'

We began to discuss my bipolar depression and how we were going to proceed. I told him about the tremors. He was concerned about my safety. We talked about adding an antidepressant, which was always dicey because I'm far more often manic than depressed. We had an off-topic conversation about the city of Boston. He knew the city, so we had a casual chat about sports teams, historical sites, and the changing atmosphere of the metropolis. He made me laugh at one point. There were smiles exchanged and we shared a few inside jokes from our long history.

Finally, we formulated a plan for moving forward. We would try an antidepressant. He'd do some blood work and look at my lithium and Depakote levels. We activated our tried and true safety plan. He told me he wanted to see me in a week, and he invited me to call him or email him through Lynn at any time. I started to recognize the person I was talking to. This physician I knew. I felt his concern, caring, and attention. What I didn't hear was any clue to the resolution of the Chuck Incident.

But at this first appointment, after the great Boston upheaval, I thought our session was perfect. I knew I would be able to return the following week. We'd taken a baby step toward normalizing our relationship that session. Maybe I was witnessing Dr. Guterson responding to my letter in his own way and at his own pace. I mouthed a "Thank you" to Rabbi Menachem as I left Dr. Guterson's office.

As one month flowed into another, our psychiatrist–patient relationship fell back into a semi-familiar pattern. My depression resolved. With medication adjustments, the hand tremors subsided. He and I slowly and tentatively found ways to communicate with each other.

However, the elephant in the room was always, at least for me, the Chuck Incident. There was guardedness in the way I spoke with Dr. Guterson. I'd become hypersensitive to abandonment once again. I found myself withholding information, just like before. There was a tiny piece of me that didn't quite believe him when he expressed empathy or concern. The doubt was subterranean, but it would bubble to the surface every now and then and, a needless crisis would erupt.

This one particular time, about a year after my Boston trip, I began having a rough road at work. Because I'd developed a rocky relationship with a volatile supervisor, I felt uncertain about my professional standing, excluded, and marginalized. This was an open invitation to a trauma response. One afternoon, a coworker came into my office and took work off my desk, matter-of-factly letting me know my services on that project were no longer wanted. I closed my office door and choked back tears. I could literally feel myself regressing. I wasn't 52 anymore; I was now three, huddled in my office corner, rocking. My adult mind said, *Don't let anyone see you like this! Call Dr. Guterson.*

Normally I would have called Lynn, but she was unavailable that day. I called him instead. He called me back in a less-than-therapeutic mood. As I tried to choke out what had gone on that afternoon, I heard the impatience in his voice mount. 'Well, you aren't on the floor now, are you? This doesn't seem urgent to me.'

His impatience translated to my traumatized ears as him telling me that I was worthless, insignificant, and a bother. I hung the phone up on him because I had to run to the restroom to vomit. My reaction to his call was that intense.

I kept praying he'd call me back and check on me. After all, I had never hung up on him before. Certainly, he could figure out something was really wrong. He never called. Chuck's cruel rant raged in my memory and the black hole that was Dr. Guterson's response to it sucked me in once again. I left the office before my day was completed. I was aware enough to know that I couldn't allow anyone to see me in that condition at work, especially given the hostility I was already encountering.

*

All of this happened on a Friday afternoon, hours before the beginning of Shabbos. There would be no chance of communication between Dr. Guterson and me for at least 25 hours. I made it home from work – suicidal, discarded, desperate, and emotionally injured. I broke Shabbos to call a suicide prevention hotline. I had never made a phone call like that before, ever, but I literally had nowhere else to turn.

The woman on the other end of the phone was superb. She verbally held me as I disjointedly sobbed my way through the whole tangled mess. Just as I had been encouraged to do in crises past, she told me to write it all down. I couldn't actually write till after the Shabbos, but after the woman at the hotline and I said conditional goodbyes, I mentally composed my email.

At nightfall, I wrote it all down. I called Lynn, weeping uncontrollably all over again. She said in a soothing voice, almost with a sigh, 'This is about Chuck, isn't it?'

I answered in my persecuted child's voice. 'Uh-huh.'

Lynn asked me to forward her the email and she'd make sure Dr. Guterson read it and responded. I said in type what I couldn't say in words. I reminded him about the new dynamics at work. I reminded him I was in deep trauma and not at my most coherent verbal self. I told him I hung up because his impatient response created an intense physical reaction. I concluded the email by beseeching him to help me understand what happened.

I sent the email, and like too many times in our recent history, I waited anxiously for a response. I received a terse and injurious reply. His comment to me was, 'I'm not going to hold your hand through every crisis. You need to do this for yourself.'

Chuck exploded in my mind again. I was just going to have to wait till my appointment in three days. I truly didn't know if I was capable of enduring any more days of Chuck's psychological violence and Dr. Guterson's hurtfulness.

Lynn came to the rescue. In the intervening days, she had a conversation with Dr. Guterson, the details of which I was not privy to. In a phone call back to me, she gave me her 100% assurance that all would be fine and to just hang tough. I hung tough and again waited till Wednesday at 6pm.

I sat curled in a ball on the upholstered chair facing Dr. Guterson, but avoiding his gaze. I wasn't crying but I felt nauseated. I said nothing. He began to speak.

Looking at me with genuine remorse, Dr. Guterson spoke sensitively to me. 'I owe you an apology, Tova. I didn't grasp what you were going through when you called me. I wasn't feeling well all weekend. I was in a rush to get ready for the Shabbos on Friday, and I was very short and impatient with you. I was wrong.'

I uncurled my body, pursed my lips, and looked at him, overcome with relief and sympathy. My words came from my depth of compassion for him. 'Sometimes I need you to be perfect so badly that I don't remember that you are a human being and can't always be perfect with me. I felt rebuffed, abandoned, and I could sense your resentment. I attributed it to how you felt about me, not what might be going on with you. I made assumptions and a difficult situation became dangerous.'

Dr. Guterson looked relieved by my words. 'We both learned something. Know, that despite my imperfections, I am committed to your healing. I am always here for you. I believe in you.'

I decided to take a stab at the central conflict between us. The moment seemed right for at least an attempt to bring up Chuck. I gingerly broached the subject. 'You know, there would have been no way I would have allowed you to admit me to the hospital. You would have had to have done it without my consent.'

Dr. Guterson looked at me genuinely surprised and asked, 'Why?'

I settled myself by taking a deep breath and cautiously responded, 'I will never consent to ever be on the same unit as Chuck. You'd have to force it.'

Dr. Guterson's inscrutable look returned. In a considered and subdued tone, he said, 'Tova, Chuck was fired.'

I gasped at the revelation, and looked at him wide-eyed. My first thought was to ask if it was because of me. I said instead, 'Thank G-d.'

Dr. Guterson made no response. He continued to have that look on his face which had, to me, come to mean complete and utter indifference.

The session ended and I felt a mixture of great relief, incredible respect for his bravery, and confusion by more unanswered Chuck questions. At least, I thought to myself, Chuck couldn't damage me or any other vulnerable patient again. I had no compassion for the man for having lost his job or the role I may have played in his firing. I despised Chuck. He had dragged me into hell and threatened the most seminal relationship in my life. I wished him only ill. I walked through the parking lot feeling triumphant. An abuser had been slain.

*

Dr. Guterson and I took a few more baby steps toward healing our bond during that session, but it would take another year and another watershed conversation for the wound to be completely bound.

In November of 2015, I awaited with great anticipation the appointment that fell on our 20th anniversary. I was bursting with thoughts to express, questions to ask, and memories to share. The questions I wanted to ask the most directly and courageously were about the Chuck Incident. Gradually and cautiously, over the two years since the trauma, I had eased myself back into the rhythm of my therapeutic relationship with him. But this dragon needed to be slain and buried.

I was two years stronger, two years more trusting, and two years healthier. I was so ready. That's not to say I wasn't uneasy, but I was confident enough in the strength of our mending bond that I knew it was time.

I started the session by reminding him that this was our 20th anniversary. He looked back into my file and said with a smile, 'You are almost correct. You're off by two days.' We both laughed at the humor of his precision. I then took the plunge.

Staring directly into his eyes, unflinching, I said, 'Dr. Guterson, there is a wound I carry that needs to be healed. Chuck. I can't move past it no matter how hard I try, without us talking about it.'

Dr. Guterson gazed at me with that look he gets when he's thoroughly engaged, that mixture of compassion and intensity. 'I want to hear about it.'

I took a deep breath and knew the moment had arrived. I said a quick prayer that the right words would flow from my lips. 'Can you please tell me why you absolutely refused to talk to me about the time when Chuck assaulted me? Remember, the summer before your dad passed away?'

Dr. Guterson looked stunned by the question, but he physically leaned into my words. He spoke in a subdued yet respectful voice. 'This must be critically important to you to have held onto it for this long.'

I composed myself and let my hurt speak for me. 'Chuck's assault devastated me, but what was more damaging was the belief that you didn't care about his abuse and did nothing to protect me when it happened.'

Dr. Guterson spoke earnestly, without a hint of defensiveness. 'Tova, I did do something. I told him that his behavior was totally unacceptable and that I was taking him off of your nursing rotation. I told him to leave you alone.'

As I listened to his words, I was also opening up to the two years of grief I had lived with. 'Then you did defend and protect me.' It was a rhetorical statement. 'Why didn't you just tell me? Why did you shut me down every time I tried to get you to talk to me about it? Why didn't you listen to my letter? Why didn't you even once ask me how I was handling the abuse?' At this point, tears were streaming down my cheeks freely.

The pain on his face was so visual; it was clear he felt terrible. 'Tova, I don't know,' he said with regret and empathy. 'Maybe I thought it would blow over. Maybe I thought it was a therapy issue. Maybe I just couldn't hear you at that time. For whatever reason, I dropped the ball.'

I had to stifle my impulse to run around his desk and hug him.

I had one more question for him though, one more crucial question. 'If you had the whole incident to do over again, what would you do differently?'

Dr. Guterson looked deeply pensive and earnest. His words were deliberate and tinged with contrition. 'I would have listened to your pain and addressed every question. I would have listened to your letter. I would have respected just how injured you were. I would never have let you suffer the aftermath of the abuse without my support.'

I could literally feel the last centimeters of the wound suture up. I let the tears of relief flow. There were no words left to be spoken, but my eyes, body language, and tears spoke for me. I was free. After two years of anguish, distrust, and dread, the Chuck Incident was over. It was time to leave Chuck in the past. The worst crisis Dr. Guterson's and my relationship had ever faced was resolved.

*

There were some powerful take-away lessons for me as I sat at home, soaking in my newfound serenity and sipping my customary cup of tea. I thought about the extraordinary anniversary gift Dr. Guterson entrusted me with. That level of humility in the face of his harmful mistake awed me. I learned that even the most trusted and nurturing bonds can be sorely tested and yet still thrive. Never again would I doubt that there were people in my life I could depend on in times of trial to not desert me.

Perseverance didn't just mean merely surviving trauma for survival's sake, as was true for most of my life. It could also mean hanging tough, because what you are hanging tough for is so precious. Not a single tear rolled down my cheek as I absorbed all that had happened over the two years since Chuck. Instead, a feeling of wellbeing permeated my core.

I felt at peace.

CHAPTER 11

Finding my Voice

One of my childhood caretakers told me a story about my three-year-old self, not long before I left for my years of Peace Corps service in 1983. It was as if she was seeking atonement for what she had witnessed. She described my unnerving ability as a toddler to sit stoically. No toys, no picture books, just huddled in a corner, silent, staring, and rocking. She wondered what could possibly have been going on inside my head that was so engrossing.

In a normal world, a baby found in my condition would set off alarm bells. However, I wasn't born into a normal world. Whatever the events in my earliest childhood were, I'll never know because my many caretakers have long since passed away. What I do know is that even at three, my own inner world must have felt much safer than the external world where the grown-ups dwelled. No one back then bothered to ask that baby anything. Dr. Guterson and Lynn were now listening for her voice. The problem was, even in middle age, she hadn't learned to speak yet.

The spoken word has always been a struggle for me. There is a disconnect between the words that so freely form in my mind and the words that flow from my lips. My journey from silence to expression has been long and tortured, but it has been life-changing.

The bridge between my thoughts and my speech has turned out to be the written word, but it wasn't always that way. My first baby steps toward self-expression began while hospitalized back in 1994. One of the required therapy groups was journaling group.

You'd think that I would take up journaling with zeal. In fact, the opposite emerged. The mantra of the group was that our writings were "private" and no therapist or clinician would ever ask to read them. In other words, I could transfer my buried thoughts, feelings, and experiences onto paper but they would still remain silent and hidden. The rage I felt at being asked to stay silent, yet again, was intense. If I was going to pour my soul into a notebook, I wanted someone on the other end, reading. From my perspective, if there was going to be no one to bear witness to my suffering and torment, there wasn't any point in wasting the considerable psychic and emotional energy needed to write the words down.

When it came to journaling, my behavior reverted to passive-aggressive fury. I was hostile, obstinate, and devious about journaling. I also procrastinated a lot. We were required to journal for three 20-minute timed sessions a day. That was an hour a day I was required to write to no one about the brutality of my life experiences. I didn't need journaling group to help me talk to no one. I was already a master at that.

My solution was to journal about the most vapid and shallow topics I could think of. I wrote about the desk in my hospital room, the most disgusting food that happened to be served to me that day, the multicolored and twirling geometric shapes that sometimes popped into my mind, or whatever random words drifted through my brain. It was an ego rush to defy these people without their knowledge. Sometimes I would involuntarily giggle in journaling group as the therapist discussed the important role writing would play in our healing. The clinicians had no idea that I was playing an elaborate game with them. Sometimes, I thought, silence was sweet revenge.

A funny thing happened as my eight months of incarceration progressed and my defiant writings piled up – I began to enjoy journaling time. There was value in creative expression. Even pointless topics had their place. Besides, it killed time in a world where time was frozen. I never was a creative writer. I was a science writer by training. From forced journaling emerged a kind of art out of madness. It would take another decade for me to find the ears willing to listen to my crafted words.

The session where I sat in Dr. Guterson's office with my yellow notepad and trembling hands, unburdening to him my long-withheld secrets, was a monumental leap forward in my healing. I had finally found that one physician who, with great compassion and empathy, was willing to bear witness to the brutality of my life experiences. Not only was he open to my words at that session, he made himself available for anything written I wanted to share afterward.

However, time constraints made opportunities for sharing limited. He was my psychiatrist, not my psychologist. I saw him twice a month for fifteen-minute sessions and more often than not, there was a crisis to resolve. Still, I managed to write to him because writing specifically to him was transformative. Lynn was always the first to listen to my thoughts. She helped me select those pieces most crucial for Dr. Guterson to hear. If an essential essay was long, I'd request extra session time, but for the most part I kept everything I read to him to seven minutes. You'd be amazed at how much you can read in seven minutes. The more I was heard and validated, the more I shared through my pen.

In 2013, my communication with Dr. Guterson entered the 21st century. He, Lynn, and I discovered a therapeutic use for email, which also saved me a lot of time. Up until that point all my writings had been on notepaper. I handwrote my essays, brought them to Lynn and then, if essential, brought them to Dr. Guterson. We used the exact same system, but in email form. I'd type my essay, send it to Lynn, we'd discuss it, and, if we both agreed Dr. Guterson should read it, Lynn would forward it to him. The great thing about this system was that I got that extra seven minutes of reading time back during my session. That meant extra time for discussion. Having time to communicate with him after a written disclosure put me a baby step closer to finding my emerging voice. Dr. Guterson was agreeable to the arrangement. He could read my essay on his timetable and have time to think through his response before our next appointment.

Dr. Guterson had a cautious relationship with email. He periodically reminded me that he couldn't practice medicine over the internet, but he recognized the value of receiving my written words in advance of sessions. He and I had certain understandings. He responded, except in rare circumstances, to my submissions in session, not in a return email. If he couldn't get to a piece of writing that week, I needed to be accepting of that. I agreed to this arrangement, although I confess, I would have loved for him to respond instantly to every submission. I needed to learn some patience though. It still hadn't sunk in that the important people in my life would acknowledge my pain, but that at the same time, boundaries were important. Having this email option allowed me the ability to express some of the most painful words I had to share, in a way that felt nonthreatening and validating. Over the years, I shared so much of my past pain, my present uncertainties, and my future hopes with Lynn and Dr. Guterson, not in baby steps but in great strides. Without the written word as my vehicle, I would have never found my voice.

All those essays and all those emails had the cumulative effect of forging absolute trust between me and Dr. Guterson. With the help of written communication, he and I had weathered the worst relationship crisis we faced in our decades together. One email at a time, we chipped away at my vault of secrets and traumas. With Lynn as our intermediary, he and I came to a place where our therapeutic relationship was again absolutely rock solid. It was time for me to begin taking the training wheels off and using my actual voice as opposed to my keyboard. One session, without any fanfare at all,

I walked in and spoke effortlessly about a traumatic event that had happened to me just that week.

*

That Saturday afternoon in late fall, I stood at a corner in our bustling Jewish community, waiting to cross the busy intersection. A man with stringy, long, gray hair banded in a ponytail sprinted urgently up to me. His body odor overwhelmed me. Frantically, in garbled speech, he pleaded with me to accept Jesus as my savior before demons possessed my soul. I backed myself up against a building as he pinned me in and warned me of the power of demons to destroy my flesh. I fell to my knees, begging him to stop. I knew all about demons. Those demons were always nipping at my consciousness, my nights, my sanity, my soul. I begged him to stop talking about THEM, and then the hysterical sobs started.

'Please,' I begged, 'I'm scared of the demons. They hurt little girls. Please, I'll be good. I'll be good. Make the demons go away without Jesus.'

The man stopped himself in mid-preach and looked at my huddled form on the sidewalk. He said nothing to me, but slowly backed up as if he was afraid of me. Strangers passed by, averting our drama and hoping no one would enlist them in the dynamic. I stayed kneeling on the sidewalk long after he had vanished, head in hand, repeating over and over again that "demons hurt little girls".

I described this encounter vividly to Dr. Guterson at our next session. Between tears and terror, I looked up at him hoping for protection, compassion, a solution. Instead, we had a very different conversation.

'Do you know that we just had a 15-minute discussion about a painful event and none of the words were written down first?'

'Oh my, I never realized that. You're right.' He pulled me out of the flashback of my street encounter with demon man, and our conversation took a very different turn. 'You know, it never even occurred to me to write this out. I mean, I was just desperate to tell you about the ranting man that backed me into a wall and knew all about THEM.'

'Why do you think that is?'

'I'm not afraid of you anymore? I think I'm growing up?'

Dr. Guterson had a completely different take on our exchange. 'No, I think you are finding your voice.'

There have been a number of times over our long relationship where I've wanted to run behind his desk and just hug him. Of course, I never have and never would, but this was one of those times. I realized the ghosts of Dr. X and Dr. Q were dead and buried, and the near-catastrophe that Chuck caused was forgiven. There was, for the first time, no malevolent, hovering third party in his office during sessions. There was Dr. Guterson, me, and whatever curve ball life had pitched to me. For the first time, there was suddenly no external force silencing me. The only person holding back my voice now was me.

*

Slowly and tentatively, I made the expedition from silence to verbal expression. Along the way, I learned I could trust, celebrate my resilience, and move into the world. My life no longer just consisted of work, treatment, and animals. I had gingerly begun to join the community of human beings and had reacquainted myself with my mending soul. I had the hope that one day I really could awaken without the shadow of my past dimming my future. I gave Dr. Guterson my hope to hang on to so many years ago. I was almost ready to take it back. He had cared for it well.

The one remaining obstacle to taking back my hope? The huddling, terrified toddler inside me. She and I would have to make peace.

CHAPTER 12

I can let go of
YOUR HAND NOW

'I'm disappointed in you, Tova. I'm really quite shocked. You are better than this.'

I let something trivial traumatize me. The event seems so small now. As I arrived for my appointment, a construction worker in Dr. Guterson's parking lot yelled at me to move my car or else it would be towed in five minutes. Still recovering from a recent manic episode, I was so rattled I moved it without paying the slightest bit of attention to where I parked it. I was on my way to see Dr. Guterson and by the time I arrived in his office I was pacing and ranting, and my thoughts were completely jumbled. After a session where the details were made a blur by the disorganization in my brain, I went off in search of my misplaced vehicle. I knew I had parked it somewhere in the bowels of North Belmont. I just didn't know where. The more I looked, the more I panicked. The more I panicked, the younger I felt. Eventually I ended up sitting cross-legged on the sidewalk, sobbing hysterically. I was three years old and I couldn't find my car, and I would be stuck in North Belmont, forever lost. There were no grown-ups, no one to help me.

I placed a desperate call to Dr. Guterson. No response. I was abandoned, lost, and trapped in North Belmont. Hopeless, that was what my situation was. Hopeless.

A stranger took pity on me and asked me what was wrong. I choked out that I had to park my car in a hurry and now I couldn't find it. He said, 'Let me see your keys.' Still little, I obeyed the grown-up. He showed me the car locator button and pressed it. I could hear my car in the distance, its insistent beep beckoning me. I thanked the stranger profusely. He asked if I needed him to help locate the beep. I said appreciatively, 'That's okay, I'm fine now. You have been so helpful.'

'Glad to help. My girlfriend loses her car all the time. Good luck.'

I drove home, stuck between feeling three and 55. I ran a red light. I never even saw it. I was so deep inside my inner world that the external world had disappeared, including traffic lights. I drove past my house for the same reason. I never saw it. Now I was lost, only blocks away from my own home. I made another desperate call to Dr. Guterson. He could fix it. I knew he could. No response. I roamed around my neighborhood for a while, maybe minutes, maybe an hour, I don't know. I heard a dog bark from a window. The bark sounded familiar. I looked up to see my house and my dog in the living room window.

My hands trembled and my eyes were still blurred with tears as I fumbled with the front door key. As I entered, the cats greeted me, but I went straight over to my dog and scratched his ears. He licked my hand and nuzzled me. He was lapping up my affection. I curled up in a ball on the couch, three, not three, three again. I called Dr. Guterson again. Three messages in one evening: excessive, I knew that, but I was so young, I needed him.

He called me back, barely hiding his exasperation. I panicked again. *Oh no, now he's mad.* I start to weep over the phone, piteously telling him my saga. He was unmoved. He said flatly, 'You were fine in my office.' *Was I fine?* I thought. *Is he right?*

I remembered pacing and babbling. I tried to replay bits of my conversation with him. I didn't feel okay. Now I knew I was really in trouble. I knew this tone of his. It wasn't pleasant to hear. I had crossed a line. Then I began apologizing over and over again. I knew somehow that I had screwed up and done something terrible. I had to fix it. I just could not quite grasp that the terrible thing was letting myself be traumatized over the trivial.

He was in clinical mode. I hate his clinical voice. I always feel scolded. He told me I had more resilience than I was showing. I kept pleading that I felt like a three-year-old. He responded firmly, 'We all have three-year-olds inside of us. Three-year-olds don't get to decide how we behave.'

Ouch, I thought. This was the moment where I needed to surrender to my psychiatrist's judgement, painful though it was. I calmed down. Sniffling, I said, 'I hate disappointing you. Will you like me tomorrow?'

'I like you right now,' he responded matter-of-factly.

Though it hurt to be chastised, I had an inkling that he was right about my behavior, and I told him so. He was pleased that I grasped his message. We talked medication, since this clearly was a trauma reaction that needed to be settled. Then he said, more gently, 'Get some sleep.'

Feeling more adult, I responded. 'You, too.'

*

I blew it that night. I lost insight, self-control, and basic problem-solving skills. I let myself be traumatized by a 20-second encounter with a construction worker. I had to do something about this. Again, I felt like a toddler. Sobbing all over again, I closed my eyes. For the first time in 55 years, I saw her. I saw my toddler. She had a tiny frame, long dark greasy hair, big brown desperate eyes, and a dirty blue polka dot dress. She was a reflection of a photo I once saw of myself at that age. She was me. I realized I had been carrying her around inside of me like extra baggage my entire life. Usually I resented her because she led me to terrifying shadow places from which I needed elaborate escape routes. This time, I looked at her and her arms reached up to me. In my voice, she said, 'Home.'

I realized she meant that I was her "home". This time, instead of being angry with her, tears streamed down my face on her behalf.

But she's me.

She's that haunting image that looks back at me piteously in the mirror. She is seared into my psyche. Her anguish is my anguish. Her pleas are my pleas. All she wanted from me was help. It took a shove from Dr. Guterson, but I offered her the help she had been screaming for for the last 52 years. I scooped her up just like I would scoop up three-year-old Katie.

However, as soon as I had her firmly in my arms, she was gone. I didn't understand. Where did she go? I was suddenly flooded with old memories, memories I did not want to relive and yet have relived over and over in the darkest moments of my life. Memories that had taunted me for decades but I refused to own. Instead I found ingenious, creative ways to shield myself from their brutality. I deflected them off my consciousness so I wouldn't have to really know them. I wouldn't have to feel them. I could just keep running.

Enough! Stop! I screamed at my own thoughts.

I took Dr. Guterson's extra medication and prepared my animals for sleep. As I lay in bed, I heard the toddler plead, 'Home,' her voice an echo now. I realized I had finally given her a home. I didn't know what that meant for me. But I knew one thing: treatment had just fast-forwarded. There was no baby step here.

Owning myself and my life experiences is an extremely lonely burden, even with Dr. Guterson's guidance. He's not the one who needed to take the toddler in his arms and nestle her. I talked to him the morning after I embraced her. I filled him in, emotionally, about the previous night's epilogue. He told me he was proud of me, but I wasn't sure I was proud of me. I felt both powerful and fragile. I knew there was more work to do, yet, the burden seemed so much lighter than just the previous afternoon.

At our next appointment, I said to Dr. Guterson, 'I've been holding on to your hands so tightly for so long. I think it's time for me to let go and take some steps on my own.'

Dr. Guterson looked at me proudly. 'You are ready to take those steps. I'll still be here, celebrating your freedom and knowing you can – and have – scaled mountains. You, indeed, can walk without holding my hand so tightly.'

It was my turn to finally feel proud. He wasn't pushing me away or abandoning me, as I might have felt just a few years prior. He was giving me permission to explore the world, unburdened, under my own power, and on my own quirky terms. As long as I have bipolar I disorder and chronic trauma, he'll still be my psychiatrist. He will, however, no longer be my sole bridge to sanity or humanity.

I have both my voice and emancipation now.

EPILOGUE

DR. GUTERSON'S OWN WORDS

In the words of the sages:

What I learned most, I learned from my students ...

Tova Feinman's story is a most remarkable journey, a journey of great courage. When Tova told me she wanted to write this book, I thought how perfect and consistent it was with her approach throughout all our therapeutic work together.

Most people seek psychiatric help at times of crisis. After a few urgent meetings, they move on or disappear – that is, of course, until the next crisis inevitably comes along. And so it goes, a merry-go-round, sadly, with little true growth or change.

The journey of therapy is work, hard work. It starts with the humility to truly look at oneself, to rein in one's ego. Next involves an uncovering of one's soul and discovering the beauty that already, inherently exists deep within us. Ultimately, however, one needs to reach outside the self, to touch and to change the world for the better.

Yes, the psychiatrist can provide guidance and care, but the journey will go nowhere without the desire, and action of the patient.

This is precisely what Tova has done here. Listen to her words. Read them carefully. Her youth and adulthood have been filled with pain and abuse of the worst dimensions. But she has been determined to get better.

Indeed, we all have difficulties in our lives. So, we have a choice: to hide away and live a life of avoidance and distraction, or to tackle the challenges with all of their inevitable pains and pitfalls. And it is through taking on these challenges that we truly grow.

For Tova, none of this could have happened without also making a connection to her soul. Certainly, knowledge of the brain, of correct medication treatment, is imperative in the psychiatric craft. But psychiatric work also needs to embrace and engage our soul, our spiritual yearning, the need for mission and meaning.

And so, I applaud and I thank Tova, for her earnestness, for her humility, for teaching me.

And now, for her gift to the world.

John Yaakov Guterson, MD (aka Dr. Guterson)

ACKNOWLEDGEMENTS

I want first to acknowledge Dr. Guterson, my psychiatrist of 22 years. He said to me, years before I even thought about writing, 'Tova, you should think about writing a book.' Little did he know that the first book I would choose to write was on the evolution of his and my clinical relationship. Dr. Guterson did the delicate balancing act of being hands off with this project while making himself available for the clinical insight I needed in order to write accurately. This book contains descriptions of some of the most intense psychiatric and medical moments we faced as physician and patient. Because of him, the book is a melding of my inner experiences and objective facts. Dr. Guterson showed a rare kind of courage as I wrote about our work. He allowed me to write with complete honesty, a rare honor.

I want to express my humble gratitude to my rebbetzin, a gifted writer in her own right. When I told Dr. Guterson my idea to write a book about our journey together, I expressed uncertainty about how to start the process of writing. He sent me straight to my rebbetzin. She was supportive, encouraging, and gave me a piece of advice I will always hang on to; to believe in my dream. Armed with her words of wisdom, I began to write.

The Creative Nonfiction Society's mentoring program provided me with the guidance and expertise I needed to craft the best book I was capable of writing. Kelsey Osgood and I were matched as mentor and mentee. Her first words to me were, 'I'm not here to compliment your writing. In fact, you will rarely get a compliment from me. My job is to help you create the best piece of work possible.' After I accepted that this was not going to be a warm and fuzzy process, I let Kelsey lead me. I was profoundly blessed to have been matched with Kelsey and over the years we've worked together, I've learned to become an author.

My psychologist, Lynn, was also instrumental in helping me sort through and clarify all the clinical events she, Dr. Guterson, and I had to navigate. If I wasn't clear about a particular event or I needed her insight into the details of an episode of illness, Lynn graciously and professionally gave me clarity, honesty, and guidance. I could not have written this book without both her and Dr. Guterson's honest recollections of some very painful moments in my treatment. I am honored that Lynn, like my psychiatrist, took the time to ensure that my description of clinical events was accurate.

When I needed to graduate from writing the manuscript to finding it a publisher, I turned to Dorit Sasson, a well-established author with a gift for marketing. Dorit's advice to me was write smaller pieces of work and get them published in online publications. I followed Dorit's advice and wrote four essays that were all accepted for publication. Her insight and advice led me to Trigger; without Dorit's expertise and drive, this book might still be sitting in my desk drawer, never seen by a potential publisher or reader.

In addition to Kelsey, Andrea Chester, a writing instructor at the Community College of Allegheny County, also provided valuable edits. When my editor at Trigger requested additions to the manuscript before it could be accepted, Andrea provided the editing and guidance I needed for those last insertions of text. Andrea was patient and insightful with my new material. I'm so grateful for her sensitivity and gentle crafting of words.

It is with great humility and profound respect that I acknowledge my editor, Kasim Mohammed, and Trigger. They saw something in my manuscript that they thought had promise and they took a chance on a new author. I had a story to tell but not much of a publishing resume. Everyone I have dealt with at Trigger has been supportive, helpful, and knowledgeable. It is an honor to be associated with such a professional group of people. They call Trigger and its authors a family. Indeed, that is exactly how it feels.

Finally, I would like to make special mention of all the tea shops I've sipped in as I crafted and discussed this book in all its phases. I dragged my laptop and my friends all over Western Pennsylvania and even into Crown Heights, New York. Every shop made me the perfect cup of tea, which motivated me to take on the next challenge in writing *Teacup in a Storm*.

.

.

Sign up to our charity, The Shaw Mind Foundation
www.shawmindfoundation.org
and keep in touch with us; we would love to hear from you.

We aim to bring to an end the suffering and despair caused by mental health issues. Our goal is to make help and support available for every single person in society, from all walks of life. We will never stop offering hope. These are our promises.